# Leckie × Leckie
Scotland's leading educational publishers

# Practice Papers for SQA Exams

## Standard Grade | General

# Chemistry

| | |
|---|---|
| Introduction | 3 |
| Topic Index | 6 |
| Exam A | 9 |
| Exam B | 35 |
| Exam C | 57 |
| Exam D | 83 |
| **Worked Answers** | **107** |

*Text* © 2009 Nicola Robertson and Douglas Robertson
*Design and layout* © 2009 Leckie & Leckie

01/150609

All rights reserved. No part of this publication may be reproduced, stored in a retrieval system, or transmitted in any form or by any means, electronic, mechanical, photocopying, recording or otherwise, without prior permission in writing from Leckie & Leckie Ltd. Legal action will be taken by Leckie & Leckie Ltd against any infringement of our copyright.

The right of Nicola Robertson and Douglas Robertson to be identified as Author of this Work has been asserted by them in accordance with sections 77 and 78 of the Copyright, Designs and Patents Act 1988.

ISBN 978-1-84372-788-0

Published by
Leckie & Leckie Ltd, 3rd floor, 4 Queen Street, Edinburgh, EH2 1JE
Tel: 0131 220 6831 Fax: 0131 225 9987
enquiries@leckieandleckie.co.uk    www.leckieandleckie.co.uk

A CIP Catalogue record for this book is available from the British Library.

Leckie & Leckie Ltd is a division of Huveaux plc.

Questions and answers in this book do not emanate from SQA. All of our entirely new and original Practice Papers have been written by experienced authors working directly for the publisher.

# Introduction

### Layout of the Book

This book contains practice exam papers, which mirror the actual SQA exam as much as possible. The layout, paper colour and question level are all similar to the actual exam that you will sit, so that you are familiar with what the exam paper will look like.

The answer section is at the back of the book. Each answer contains a worked-out answer or solution so that you can see how the right answer has been arrived at. The answers also include practical tips on how to tackle certain types of questions, details of how marks are awarded and advice on just what the examiners will be looking for.

Revision advice is provided in this introductory section of the book, so please read on!

### How To Use This Book

The Practice Papers can be used in two main ways:

1. You can complete an entire practice paper as preparation for the final exam. If you would like to use the book in this way, you can either complete the practice paper under exam-style conditions by setting yourself a time for each paper and answering it as well as possible without using any references or notes. The general exam is one and half hours long. Try to find a quiet place where you will not be disturbed if you want to try the paper under exam conditions. Alternatively, you can answer the practice paper questions as a revision exercise, using your notes to produce a model answer. Your teacher may mark these for you.

2. You can use the Topic Index at the back of this book to find all the questions within the book that deal with a specific topic. This allows you to focus specifically on areas that you particularly want to revise or, if you are mid-way through your course, it lets you practise answering exam-style questions for just those topics that you have studied.

### Revision Advice

Work out a revision timetable for each week's work in advance – remember to cover all of your subjects and to leave time for homework and breaks. For example:

| Day | 6pm–6.45pm | 7pm–8pm | 8.15pm–9pm | 9.15pm–10pm |
|---|---|---|---|---|
| Monday | Homework | Homework | English revision | Chemistry revision |
| Tuesday | Maths revision | Physics revision | Homework | Free |
| Wednesday | Geography revision | Modern Studies revision | English revision | French revision |
| Thursday | Homework | Maths revision | Chemistry revision | Free |
| Friday | Geography revision | French revision | Free | Free |
| Saturday | Free | Free | Free | Free |
| Sunday | Modern Studies revision | Maths revision | Modern Studies revision | Homework |

Make sure that you have at least one evening free a week to relax, socialise and re-charge your batteries. It also gives your brain a chance to process the information that you have been feeding it all week.

Arrange your study time into sessions of 30 minutes or 1 hour, with a break between sessions e.g. 6pm–7pm, 7.15pm–7.45pm, 8pm–9pm. Try to start studying as early as possible in the evening when your brain is still alert and be aware that the longer you put off starting, the harder it will be to start!

Study a different subject in each session, except for the day before an exam.

Do something different during your breaks between study sessions – have a cup of tea, or listen to some music. Don't let your 15 minutes expanded into 20 or 25 minutes though!

Have your class notes, any textbooks and learning outcomes available for your revision to hand as well as plenty of blank paper, a pen, etc. Learning outcomes will help you to focus your revision on what you need to learn. You may like to make keyword sheets like the chemistry example below:

| Keyword | Meaning |
|---|---|
| alkali metal | Metal in group 1 of the Periodic Table |
| biodegradable | Able to rot away by natural biological processes |
| compound | A substance which has two or more elements joined together. |

In Chemistry there are many reactions to learn, so it may be useful to make a list, like the example below:

| Reaction | Meaning |
|---|---|
| addition | When a molecule such as hydrogen or bromine 'adds on' across the double C=C bond in an unsaturated hydrocarbon such as ethene. |
| combustion | Burning a substance in oxygen |
| exothermic | A reaction in which energy is given out. |

Finally forget or ignore all or some of the advice in this section if you are happy with your present way of studying. Everyone revises differently, so find a way that works for you!

## Transfer Your Knowledge

As well as using your class notes, textbooks and learning outcomes to revise, these practice papers will also be a useful revision tool as they will help you to get used to answering exam-style questions. The exam questions are split into two types – knowledge and understanding (KU) and problem solving (PS). You can look in the marks column at the side of the question to see if a question is KU or PS. A knowledge and understanding question is asking for a piece of knowledge you have learned. In a problem-solving question you must either work the answer out or you may have to apply some of your knowledge. You may find as you work through the questions that some problem-solving questions use an example that you haven't come across before. Don't worry! You should be able to transfer your knowledge of a topic to a new example. The enhanced answer section at the back will demonstrate how to read and interpret the question to identify the topic being examined and how to apply your course knowledge in order to answer the question successfully.

## Command Words

In the practice papers and in the exam itself, a number of command words will be used in the questions. These command words are used to show you how you should answer a question – some words indicate that you should write more than others. If you familiarise yourself with these command words, it will help you to structure your answers more effectively.

| Command Word | Meaning/Explanation |
|---|---|
| Identify | Used in the grid section. Basically you have to pick an answer or answers from a selection of choices.<br><br>e.g. **Identify** the metal that is extracted in the blast furnace. |
| Name or term | Usually one short answer is required.<br><br>e.g. **Name** an essential element provide by fertilisers<br>What **term** is used to describe this type of plastic? |
| State | Usually requires a slightly longer answer.<br><br>e.g. **State** the test for carbon dioxide |

| Suggest | Could be one answer or an idea you are being asked for |
| --- | --- |
| | e.g. **suggest** a voltage… |
| | **suggest** an advantage… |
| Describe | Give a bit more more detail |
| | **Describe** how you would use pH paper to test the pH of a solution. |
| Explain | This is asking you for a reason why something has happened. |
| | e.g. **Explain** why there has been an increased us of fertilisers in the last 100 years. |
| Predict | Make a prediction based on data given in a table or chart. |

## In the Exam

Watch your time and pace yourself carefully. Work out roughly how much time you can spend on each answer and try to stick to this. In the General Chemistry exam you are given one and half hours. This works out as one and a half minutes per question. Clearly some questions will take longer than others.

Be clear before the exam what the instructions are likely to be, e.g. how many questions you should answer in each section. The practice papers will help you to become familiar with the exam's instructions.

The Chemistry exam is split into two sections:

Part 1–Grid section (20 marks) (Do not spend any longer than half an hour on this section. It should take less time than this in practice.)

The grid section is a like a multiple choice, where you have to pick answers from a selection given. Grid questions only have one answer, unless stated otherwise in the question. You will always be told if you are required to give two answers. No half marks are given for the grid questions. Always put the correct number of answers even if you have to guess. You might get lucky!

Part 2–Written section (40 marks)

Both the grid section and the written section contain a mixture of knowledge and understanding and problem-solving questions. Look at the space for the marks to see what type of question it is.

Read the question thoroughly before you begin to answer it – make sure you know exactly what the question is asking you to do. If the question is in sections e.g. 15a, 15b, 15c, etc., make sure that you can answer each section before you start writing.

Plan your answer by jotting down keywords, mnemonics, word equations or any working you think will help. You can write anywhere on the exam as long as you make your final answer clear. Don't repeat the question, try to **answer** the question.

Use the resources provided. In some questions you can use the data booklet to help you. This is an extremely important book, which contains the Periodic Table and other valuable information. You will be provided with one in the exam. Make sure you are familiar with its contents. Some questions will direct you to a page you can use to help you answer the question. Some questions have diagrams, tables or graphs. Useful information from these can help you answer the question.

You should check over all your answers once you finish the paper. Don't leave any blanks. Always attempt to write something for each question.

Take a pencil and ruler into the exam to draw graphs, and a calculator in case there is a maths question.

## Topic Index

The following is a list of where in the SQA course each question comes from.

| SQA Topic | Exam A | Exam B | Exam C | Exam D |
|---|---|---|---|---|
| Chemical Reactions | 4a, 8b, 10bi | 2a | 3a, 15a, 15bii | 11a |
| Speed of Reactions | 11ai | 15a, 15cii | 19biii, 21ai | 2, 5a |
| Atoms and the Periodic Table | 1c | 1b, 1d, 4b, 10a, 10b | 1a, 10a, 10b | 1a, 4a, 4b, 4c |
| How Atoms Combine* | 4b | 4c | 1d, 20b | 11bii |
| Fuels | 5a, 5d, 6, 9a, 9b, 13d | 3c, 7a, 15b, 18b, 19a | 8a, 11ai, 11aii, 17aii | 1b, 5b, 9b, 17a |
| Hydrocarbons | 2a, 2b, 2c, 11bi, 11bii | 2c, 3a, 18ci, 18cii | 2a, 2c, 11b, 21aii | 3a, 3b, 10a, 10bi, 10bii |
| Properties of Substances** | 18a, 18b, 18c | 14a, 14b, 14c, 14d | 9, 5c | 18a, 18b, 18c, 18d |
| Acids and Alkalis | 9c, 16a, 16b | 2b, 8, 16c, 19ci | 4a, 4b, 20aii | 6a, 13a, 13bi, 13bii |
| Reactions of Acids | 5b, 14ai, 14b | 2b, 6a, 6b, 7b | 15bi, 17ai | 12b, 16ai, 16aii |
| Making Electricity | 8a, 15ai, 15aii, 15b | 12a, 12b | 12d, 18a, 18b, 18c | 7a, 7b |
| Metals | 10bii, 10c | 1c, 16a, 16b, 16c | 7, 14a, 14b | 1d, 6b |
| Corrosion | 1b, 7 | 17ai, 17aii, 17b | 1b, 6 | 14bi, 14bii |
| Plastics | 12b, 12d | 9a, 9b, 9c, 13ai | 5b, 16a, 16b, 16c | 9c, 10c |
| Fertilisers | 14c, 17ai, 17b, 17c | 4a, 13aii, 13b | 3b, 20ai | 5c, 6c, 15ai, 15b |
| Carbohydrates | 5c, 8c, 13a, 13b, 13c | 3b, 7c, 11a, 11bii | 5a, 8b, 19a, 19bi, 19bii | 8, 11bi |
| Writing Formulae | 14aii, 16c | 11c | 13b, 21bi, 21bii | 15aii, 16b |
| Writing equations | | | 12c | 11c |

*Includes molecules and covalent bonding.

**Includes ionic bonding, properties of elements, ionic and covalent compounds.

There are a number of questions that are not necessarily related to topics but rely entirely on problem-solving skills learned throughout the course. These are some of areas that are tested.

| Problem-solving Skill | Exam A | Exam B | Exam C | Exam D |
| --- | --- | --- | --- | --- |
| Drawing a bar graph | 10a | 18a | 13a | 14a |
| Fair testing | 3, 11aii | 5a | 17b | 17bii |
| Labelling a pie chart |  | 12c |  | 14c |
| Making a prediction |  | 19bi | 14c | 12c |
| Making a table using information given | 12c | 11bi |  | 9a |
| Making generalisations | 17aii | 9b | 15c | 17bi |
| Reading directly from the Data Booklet | 1a, 1d | 1a, 1b, 1d | 1a, 1c, 2b | 1c, 13c |
| Reading information from a graph |  | 15ci |  |  |
| Using a flowchart | 12a |  | 12a | 12a |
| Maths calculation |  |  | 12b |  |

# Exam A

# Chemistry

## Standard Grade: General

Practice Papers
For SQA Exams

Exam A

**Fill in these boxes:**

Name of centre

Town

Forename(s)

Surname

You have 1 hour 30 minutes to complete this paper.

Try to answer all of the questions in the time allowed.

You will find data you need in the SQA Data Booklet.

You may answer questions in any order but you must write your answers in this book, in ink, and clearly label them.

Rough work should also be done in this book, but clearly crossed out.

Leckie × Leckie
Scotland's leading educational publishers

# PART 1

**A total of 20 marks is available in part one of the paper.**

1. Some common non-metals are shown below.

| A | B | C |
|---|---|---|
| chlorine | argon | oxygen |
| **D** | **E** | **F** |
| phosphorus | carbon | fluorine |

(a) Identify the non-metal that has the symbol C.

You can refer to page 8 of the data booklet to assist you.

| A | B | C |
|---|---|---|
| D | E | F |

(b) Identify the non-metal that is required for rusting.

| A | B | C |
|---|---|---|
| D | E | F |

(c) Identify the non-metal that is very unreactive.

| A | B | C |
|---|---|---|
| D | E | F |

(d) Identify the non-metal discovered in 1774.

You can refer to page 8 of the data booklet to assist you.

| A | B | C |
|---|---|---|
| D | E | F |

*Page 12*

2. The grid contains the names of some hydrocarbons.

| A ethene | B propane | C pentene |
|---|---|---|
| D butane | E ethane | F hexane |

(a) Identify the hydrocarbon with **four** carbons in each molecule.

| A | B | C |
|---|---|---|
| D | E | F |

(b) Identify the hydrocarbon with the lowest boiling point.

You can refer to page 6 of the data booklet to assist you.

| A | B | C |
|---|---|---|
| D | E | F |

(c) Identify which **two** hydrocarbons are alkenes.

| A | B | C |
|---|---|---|
| D | E | F |

**3.** A student studied the effect of reacting chalk with acid.

He kept the volume of acid the same in each experiment.

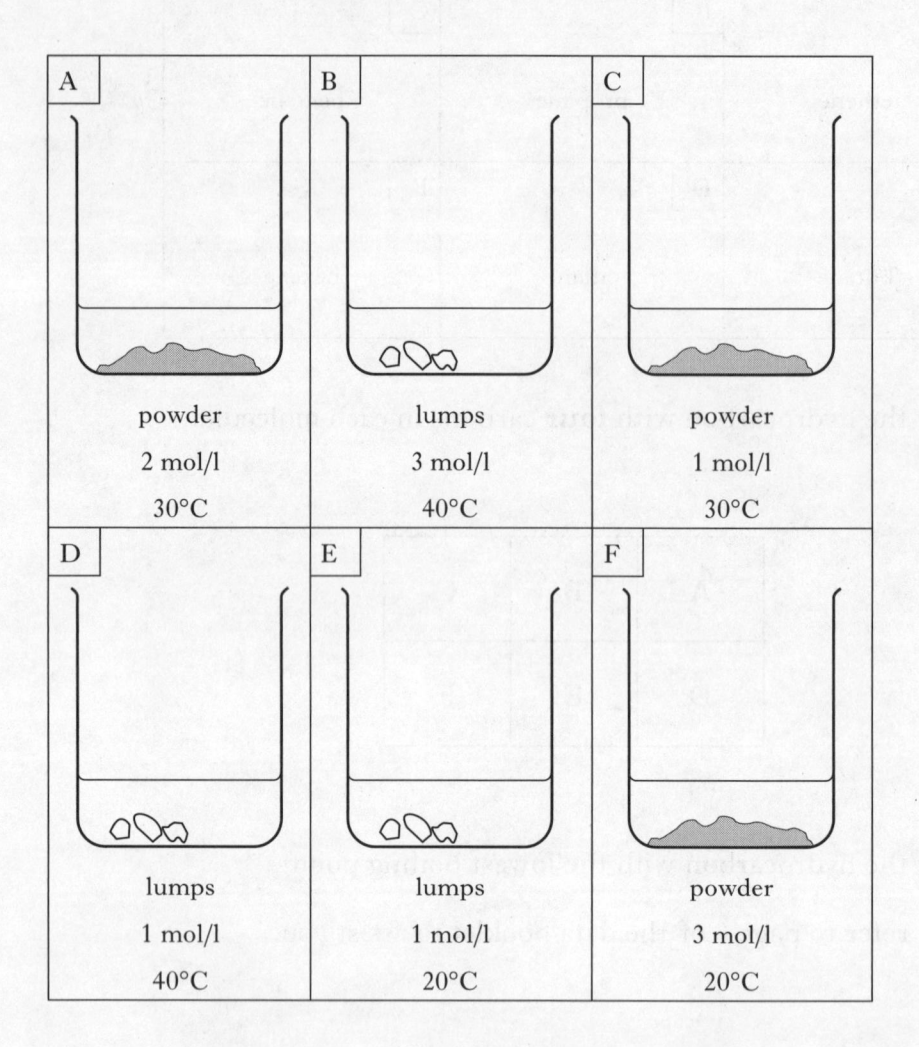

| A | B | C |
|---|---|---|
| powder | lumps | powder |
| 2 mol/l | 3 mol/l | 1 mol/l |
| 30°C | 40°C | 30°C |
| D | E | F |
| lumps | lumps | powder |
| 1 mol/l | 1 mol/l | 3 mol/l |
| 40°C | 20°C | 20°C |

Identify the **two** experiments that could be used to show how temperature affects the rate of reaction.

| A | B | C |
|---|---|---|
| D | E | F |

4. Many substances can be represented by simple diagrams like the ones shown below.

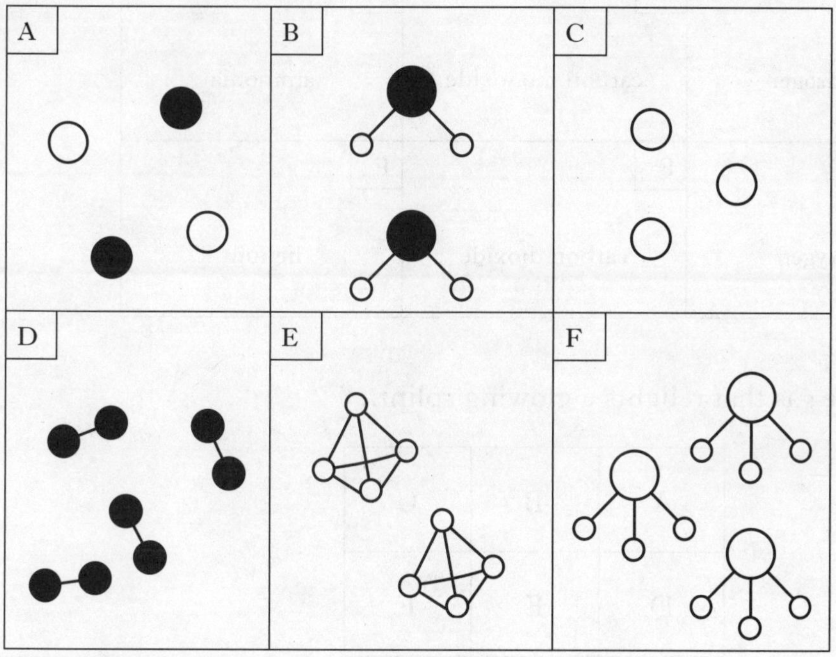

(a) Identify the **two** diagrams that represent compounds.

| A | B | C |
|---|---|---|
| D | E | F |

(b) Identify the diagram that represents **diatomic** molecules.

| A | B | C |
|---|---|---|
| D | E | F |

5. Some gases are shown below.

| A hydrogen | B carbon monoxide | C ammonia |
|---|---|---|
| D oxygen | E carbon dioxide | F helium |

(a) Identify the gas that relights a glowing splint.

| A | B | C |
|---|---|---|
| D | E | F |

(b) Identify the gas produced when acid reacts with a metal carbonate.

| A | B | C |
|---|---|---|
| D | E | F |

(c) Identify the gas that is **produced** during photosynthesis.

| A | B | C |
|---|---|---|
| D | E | F |

(d) Identify the gas that is produced during the **incomplete** combustion of a hydrocarbon.

| A | B | C |
|---|---|---|
| D | E | F |

6. Crude oil can be separated into fractions using fractional distillation.

   The table shows the boiling range of each fraction.

   | Fraction | Boiling Range/°C |
   |----------|------------------|
   | Fraction 1 | Below 20 |
   | Fraction 2 | 20–175 |
   | Fraction 3 | 150–240 |
   | Fraction 4 | 240–350 |
   | Fraction 5 | Above 350 |

   Identify the correct statement.

   | A | Fraction 1 is the most flammable. |
   |---|-----------------------------------|
   | B | Fraction 4 is more flammable than fraction 3. |
   | C | Fraction 3 will evaporate more easily than fraction 1. |
   | D | Fraction 4 is less viscous than fraction 2. |

**7.** Jessica was investigating the rusting of iron keys.

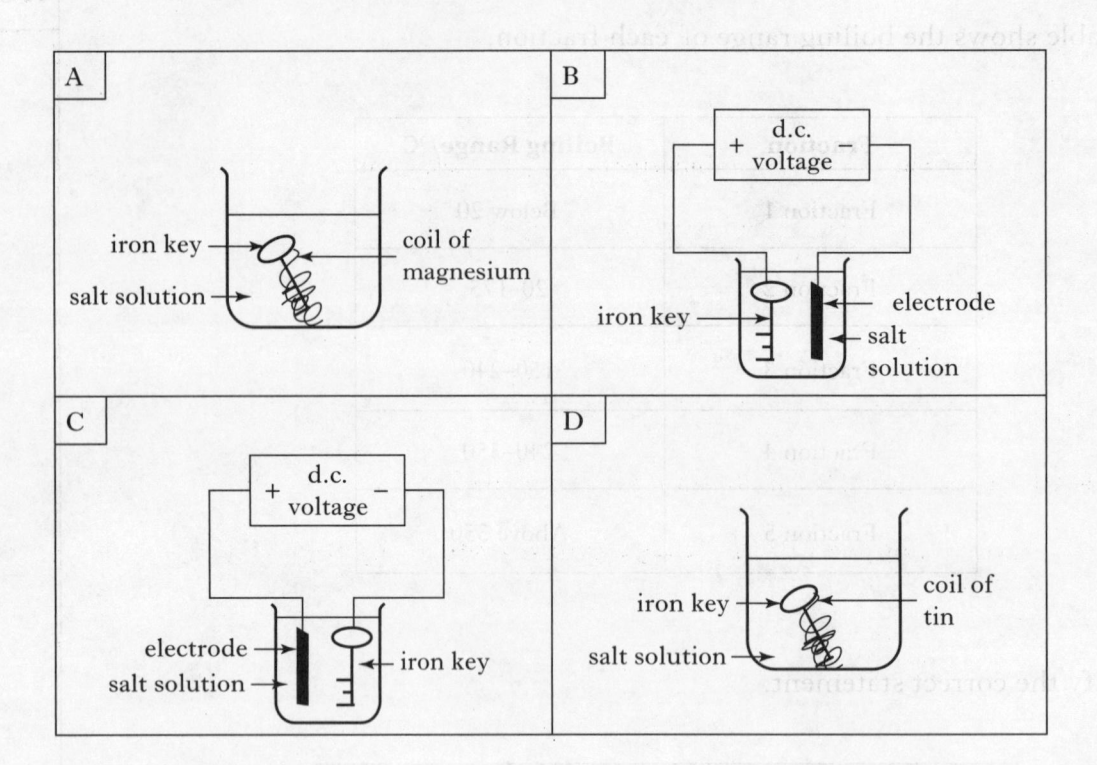

| A | B |
|---|---|
| iron key in salt solution with coil of magnesium | iron key and electrode in salt solution connected to d.c. voltage (iron key to +, electrode to −) |

| C | D |
|---|---|
| electrode and iron key in salt solution connected to d.c. voltage (electrode to +, iron key to −) | iron key in salt solution with coil of tin |

Identify the **two** experiments in which the key would be protected from rusting.

| A | B |
|---|---|
| C | D |

8. The grid shows the names of some chemical processes and reactions.

| A filtration | B combustion | C displacement |
|---|---|---|
| D fermentation | E electrolysis | F neutralisation |

(a) Identify the chemical reaction that is represented by this equation.

**iron + copper nitrate ⟶ iron nitrate + copper**

| A | B | C |
|---|---|---|
| D | E | F |

(b) Identify the process that is **not** a chemical reaction.

| A | B | C |
|---|---|---|
| D | E | F |

(c) Identify the process that requires an enzyme in yeast to act as a catalyst.

| A | B | C |
|---|---|---|
| D | E | F |

## PART 2

**A total of 40 marks is available in this part of the paper.**

9. Coal, oil and gas are finite resources, which are burned in power stations.

    (a) What is meant by a **finite** resource?

    _____

    _____

    (b) Describe how coal was formed.

    _____

    _____

    _____

    _____

    (c) Burning fossil fuels can contribute to pollution such as acid rain.

    Name a gas that causes acid rain.

    _____

**10.** Iron is extracted from iron ore.

The table shows approximately how much iron ore some countries produced in 2006.

| Country | Production of iron ore/million tonnes |
|---------|---------------------------------------|
| Ukraine | 73 |
| USA | 54 |
| Canada | 33 |
| Sweden | 24 |
| Iran | 20 |

(a) Using the graph paper below, create a bar chart that illustrates the information in the table.

*Remember to use appropriate scales when drawing the bar chart.*

| KU | PS |
|---|---|

(*b*) Iron is extracted from iron ore in a blast furnace and then used to make steel.

Part of the process is shown below:

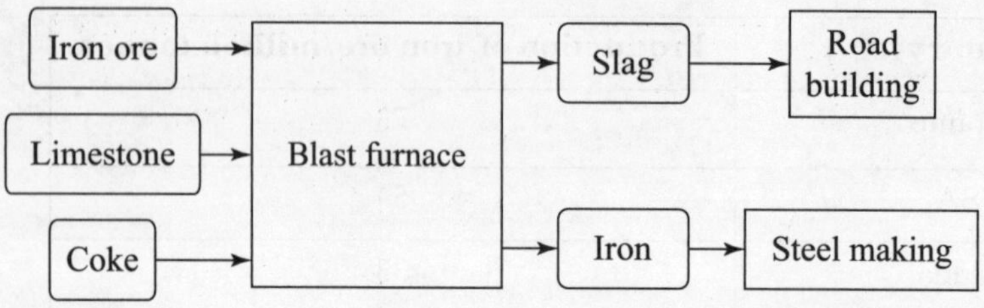

Iron ore
Limestone
Coke
Blast furnace
Slag
Road building
Iron
Steel making


(i) Limestone is used to remove any impurities from the iron ore.

Limestone is mainly composed of calcium carbonate.

Name the elements present in calcium carbonate.

__________________________________________________ 1

(ii) Alloys of iron are called steels.

What is an alloy?

__________________________________________________ 1

(*c*) Iron reacts with dilute acid to produce hydrogen gas.

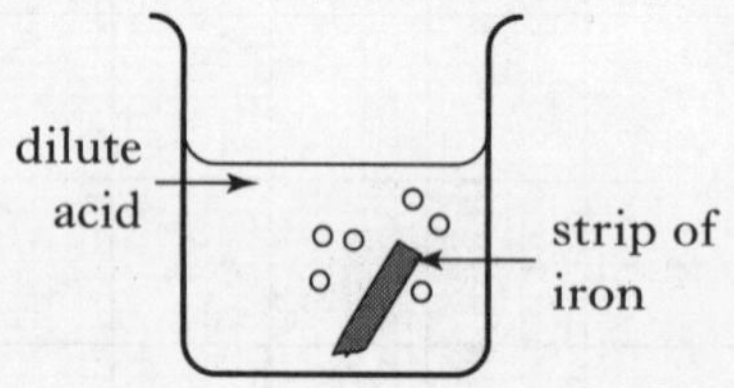

dilute acid
strip of iron


What difference would be seen if the experiment was repeated using zinc?

You can refer to page 7 of the data booklet to assist you.

__________________________________________________ 1

**11.** Richard investigated which catalyst was the best at breaking down hydrogen peroxide, using the apparatus shown below.

He measured the volume of gas produced after 30 seconds.

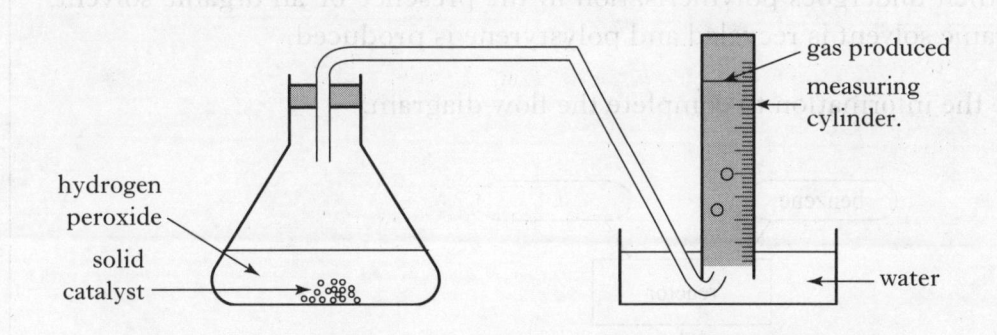

| Catalyst | Volume of gas produced after 30 s/cm³ |
|---|---|
| manganese dioxide | 15 |
| copper oxide | 11 |
| lead oxide | 8 |
| silver oxide | 4 |

(a) (i) Using the information in the table, name the catalyst that is the best at breaking down hydrogen peroxide.

(ii) Suggest a variable that Richard would have kept the same to make a fair comparison.

(b) A catalyst is used in the breakdown of hydrocarbons.

(i) Name the process used to breakdown larger hydrocarbons into smaller, more useful ones.

(ii) The equation shows the breakdown of the hydrocarbon heptane.

$$C_7H_{16} \rightarrow X + C_2H_4$$

Write the molecular formula for hydrocarbon X.

**12.** Manufacture of polystyrene

To make polystyrene, first of all benzene is reacted with ethene in a reactor to produce ethylbenzene. This is converted to styrene in a catalytic reactor. The styrene then undergoes polymerisation in the presence of an organic solvent. The organic solvent is recycled and polystyrene is produced.

(a) Use the information to complete the flow diagram.

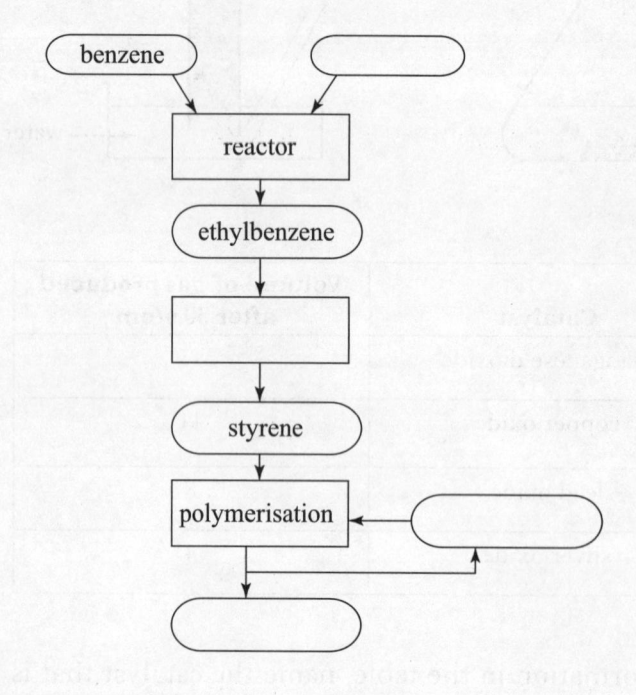

```
benzene        ( ethene )
     \         /
      → reactor ←
           ↓
      ethylbenzene
           ↓
      [ catalytic reactor ]
           ↓
        styrene
           ↓
      polymerisation ← ( organic solvent )
           ↓                    ↑
      ( polystyrene ) ──────────
```

(b) When heated, polystyrene melts and can be reshaped.

What term is used to describe such a plastic?

_____

(c) Polystyrene has many uses.

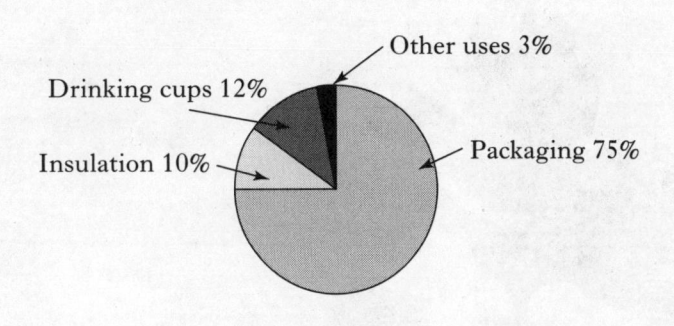

[Pie chart showing: Packaging 75%, Drinking cups 12%, Insulation 10%, Other uses 3%]

Put this information into a table with suitable headings.

| Use | Percentage (%) |
| --- | --- |
| Packaging | 75 |
| Drinking cups | 12 |
| Insulation | 10 |
| Other uses | 3 |

(d) There is a concern about the fumes produced when polystyrene burns.

Why are the fumes a health hazard?

_____

**13.** Glucose and starch are both substances made by green plants.

(a) To which family of compounds do starch and glucose belong to?

(b) Name the solution that could be used to test for glucose.

(c) Mrs Clark demonstrated an experiment in which a beam of light was shone through a solution of glucose and a solution of starch.

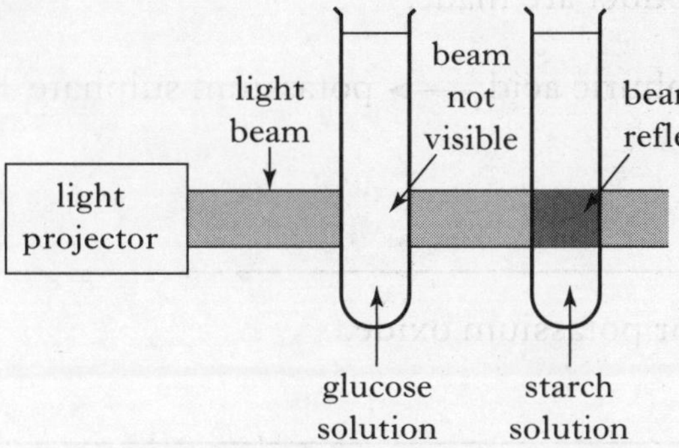

Why does the beam reflect off the starch solution, but not off the glucose solution?

_____

_____

(d) When burned, both starch and glucose release heat energy.

What term describes reactions that release heat energy?

_____

14. Potassium oxide is a compound found in some fertilisers.

(a) When potassium oxide is reacted with dilute sulphuric acid, potassium sulphate and another product are made.

  potassium oxide + sulphuric acid ⟶ potassium sulphate + product A

 (i) Name product A.

 _____

 (ii) Write the formula for potassium oxide.

 _____

(b) Potassium sulphate can be reacted with barium chloride to form a solid.

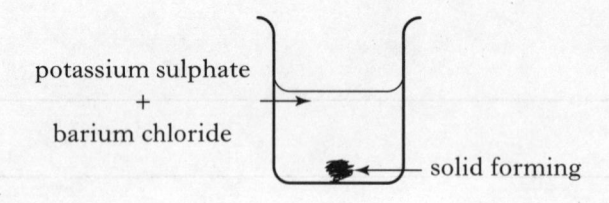

   potassium sulphate + barium chloride → solid forming

 Name the solid formed.

 You may wish to use page 5 of the data booklet to help you.

 _____

(c) Suggest why potassium oxide is found in some fertilisers.

 _____

**15.** A battery manufacturer was trying to design a new cell. They had two suggestions.

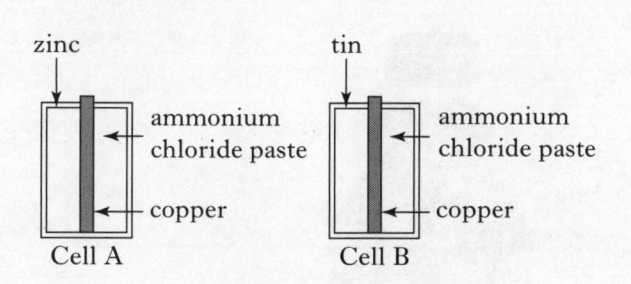

*(a)* (i) In cell A, which way do the electrons flow?

Circle the correct answer.

$$\begin{Bmatrix} \text{zinc to copper} \\ \text{copper to zinc} \end{Bmatrix}$$

You may wish to use page 7 of the data booklet to help you.

(ii) Which cell, A or B, would give the greatest voltage?

You can refer to page 7 of the data booklet to assist you.

_____

*(b)* What is the purpose of the ammonium chloride paste?

_____

**16.** The pH of an orange drink was tested and found to be acidic with a pH of 4.

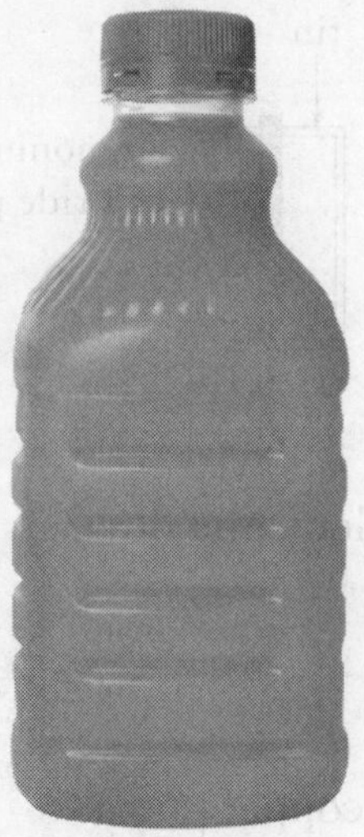

(a) The drink was diluted by adding water to it.

Predict its pH after dilution

pH _____

(b) Name the **ion** which causes solutions to be acidic

_____

(c) The acid present in fruit juice is citric acid. Its structure is shown below.

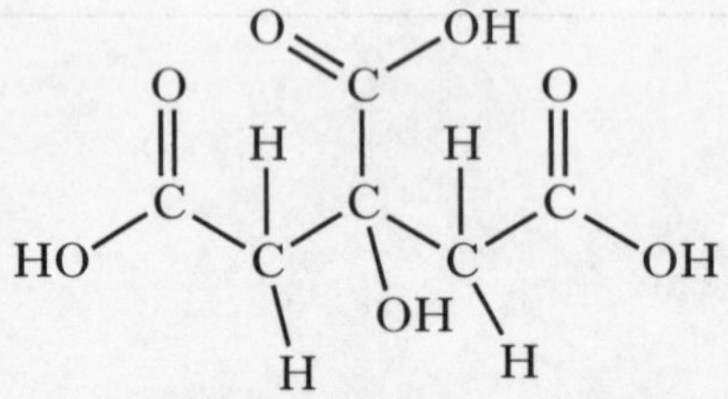

Complete the formula to show the number of each type of atom in citric acid.

# C     H     O

**17.** The Haber process is used to make the gas ammonia from nitrogen and hydrogen.

(a) (i) Name the catalyst used in this process

_____

(ii) The percentage yield of ammonia produced depends on the pressure used.

The graph shows the % yield of ammonia at different pressures.

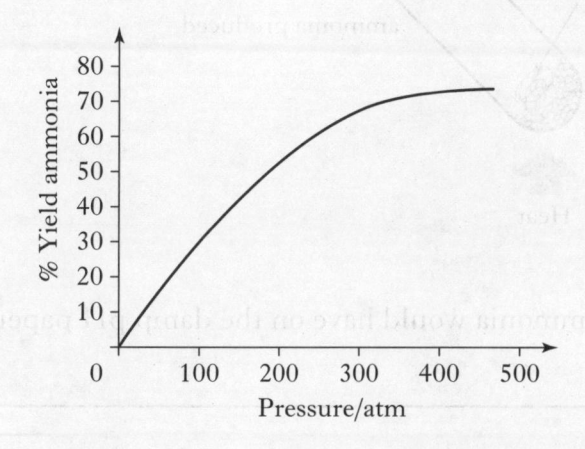

Describe the general trend in the % yield of ammonia when the pressure increases.

_____

_____

(b) Ammonia is used in the making of fertiliser.

Explain why there has been increased demanded for fertilisers during the last 100 years.

_____

_____

_____

(c) A chemistry teacher cut off a little of her hair and heated it with soda lime in a test tube. Ammonia gas was produced

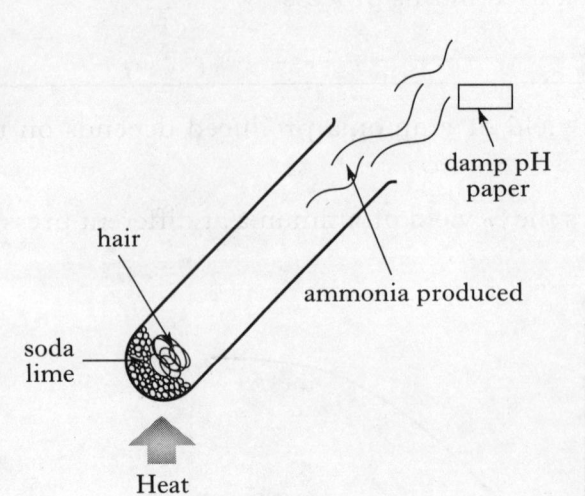

Describe the effect ammonia would have on the damp pH paper.

_____

1

**18.** A gel containing the blue chemical copper chloride was electrolysed.

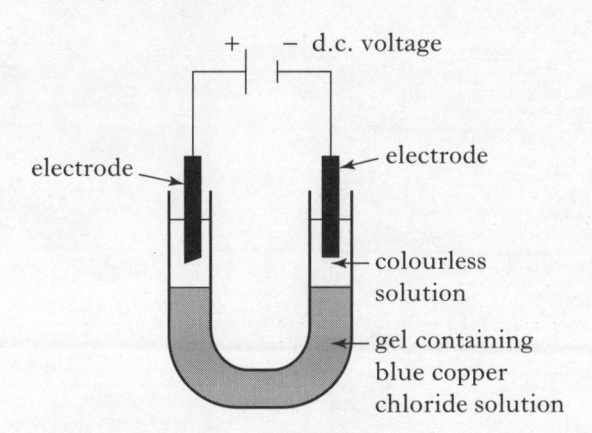

*(a)* Suggest a non-metal that could be used to make the electrodes.

*(b)* What is meant by electrolysis?

*(c)* After one hour the blue colour was only found at the negative electrode. The gel around the positive electrode was colourless.

What does this tell us about the colour of chloride ions?

[End of Question Paper]

# Exam B

**Chemistry**  Standard Grade: General

Practice Papers
For SQA Exams                                                      Exam B

**Fill in these boxes:**

Name of centre                                    Town

Forename(s)                                       Surname

You have 1 hour 30 minutes to complete this paper.

Try to answer all of the questions in the time allowed.

You will find data you need in the SQA Data Booklet.

You may answer questions in any order but you must write your answers in this book, in ink, and clearly label them.

Rough work should also be done in this book, but clearly crossed out.

**Leckie×Leckie**
Scotland's leading educational publishers

## PART 1

**A total of 20 marks is available in this part of the paper.**

1. The grid contains the names of some metals.

   | A | B | C |
   |---|---|---|
   | plutonium | potassium | lithium |
   | D | E | F |
   | iron | silver | magnesium |

   (a) Identify the metal that gives a red flame colour.

   You can refer to page 4 of the data booklet to assist you.

   | A | B | C |
   |---|---|---|
   | D | E | F |

   (b) Identify the metal that was discovered by scientists.

   You can refer to page 8 of the data booklet to assist you.

   | A | B | C |
   |---|---|---|
   | D | E | F |

   (c) Identify the metal that is produced in the blast furnace.

   | A | B | C |
   |---|---|---|
   | D | E | F |

   (d) Identify the **two** transition metals.

   You can refer to page 8 of the data booklet to assist you.

   | A | B | C |
   |---|---|---|
   | D | E | F |

**2.** The grid shows the names of some substances.

| A | B | C |
|---|---|---|
| copper | sodium chloride | glucose |
| D | E | F |
| chlorine | methane | lime |

(a) Identify the **two** elements.

| A | B | C |
|---|---|---|
| D | E | F |

(b) Identify the substance that can be used to neutralise acidic soil.

| A | B | C |
|---|---|---|
| D | E | F |

(c) Identify the hydrocarbon.

| A | B | C |
|---|---|---|
| D | E | F |

**3.** The grid shows the names of some solutions.

| A bromine solution | B ferroxyl indicator | C universal indicator |
|---|---|---|
| D salt solution | E Benedict's solution | F lime water |

(a) Identify the solution that could be used to test for an unsaturated hydrocarbon.

| A | B | C |
|---|---|---|
| D | E | F |

(b) Identify the solution used to test for glucose.

| A | B | C |
|---|---|---|
| D | E | F |

(c) Identify the solution that is used to test for carbon dioxide.

| A | B | C |
|---|---|---|
| D | E | F |

**4.** Some elements are gases.

| A argon | B neon | C oxygen |
|---|---|---|
| D hydrogen | E fluorine | F chlorine |

(a) Identify the gas that reacts with nitrogen to form ammonia in the Haber process.

| A | B | C |
|---|---|---|
| D | E | F |

(b) Identify the gas that has atoms with six outer electrons.

You can refer to page 1 of the data booklet to assist you.

| A | B | C |
|---|---|---|
| D | E | F |

(c) Identify the **two** gases that do **not** exist as diatomic molecules.

| A | B | C |
|---|---|---|
| D | E | F |

5. A reaction between dilute sulphuric acid and magnesium can be set up as shown.

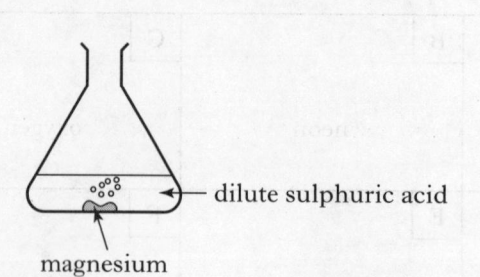

— dilute sulphuric acid
magnesium

The reaction was carried out several times using the same mass of magnesium and the same volume of acid.

|   | Temperature/°C | Concentration of sulphuric acid/mol/l | Particle size of magnesium |
|---|---|---|---|
| A | 20 | 0.5 | lumps |
| B | 40 | 0.5 | powder |
| C | 30 | 1 | lumps |
| D | 40 | 1 | lumps |
| E | 30 | 1.5 | powder |
| F | 20 | 2 | lumps |

Identify the **two** experiments that should be compared to show the effect of concentration of acid on the speed of reaction.

A
B
C
D
E
F

1

**6.** The grid contains some ionic solutions.

| A | B |
|---|---|
| ammonium carbonate | copper sulphate |
| C | D |
| sodium chloride | potassium nitrate |

(a) Identify the solution that would produce a gas when added to dilute acid.

| A | B |
|---|---|
| C | D |

(b) Identify the **two** solutions that, when mixed, produce a precipitate.

You can refer to page 5 of the data booklet to assist you.

| A | B |
|---|---|
| C | D |

**7.** The grid shows some experiments carried out by pupils in their Chemistry class.

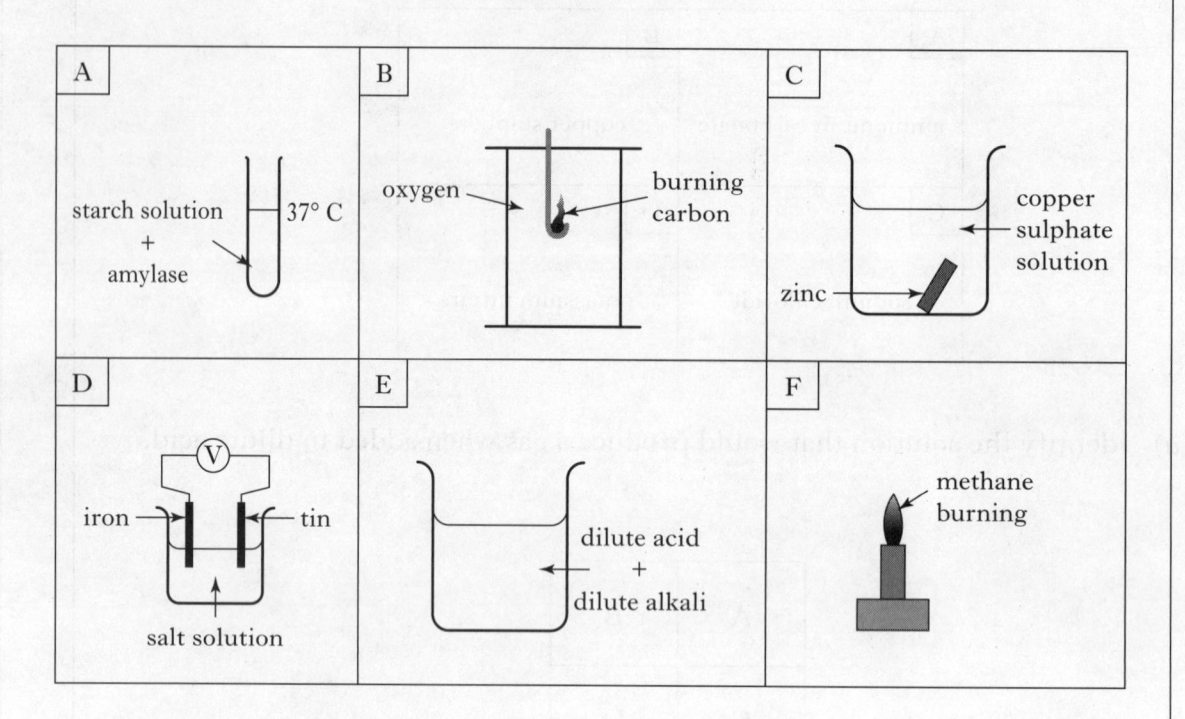

| A | B | C |
|---|---|---|
| starch solution + amylase, 37°C | oxygen, burning carbon | zinc, copper sulphate solution |

| D | E | F |
|---|---|---|
| iron — tin, salt solution (V) | dilute acid + dilute alkali | methane burning |

(a) Identify the experiment that will produce carbon dioxide **and** water as products.

| A | B | C |
|---|---|---|
| D | E | F |

(b) Identify the experiment in which neutralisation is taking place.

| A | B | C |
|---|---|---|
| D | E | F |

(c) Identify the experiment in which an enzyme is being used.

| A | B | C |
|---|---|---|
| D | E | F |

8. James set up the following circuit.

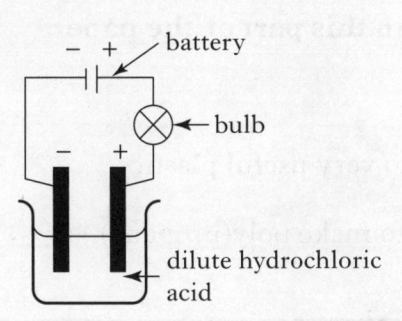

Identify the correct statement.

| A | The circuit will not conduct electricity. |
|---|---|
| B | The pH of the solution will be above 7. |
| C | There are no ions in the solution. |
| D | Hydrogen gas will be produced at the negative electrode. |

## PART 2

**A total of 40 marks is available in this part of the paper.**

9. Poly(propene) and PVC are two very useful plastics.

   (a) Name the monomer used to make poly(propene).

   _____

   (b) Poly(propene) is a thermoplastic.

   What is meant by this term?

   _____

   (c) PVC is used to cover electrical wires.

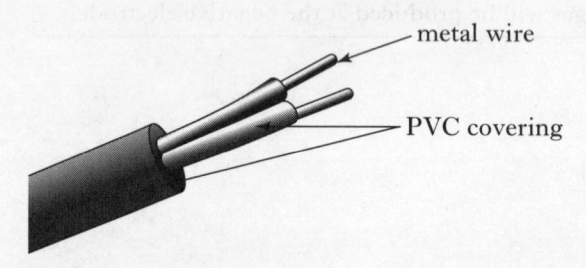

   — metal wire
   — PVC covering

   Suggest a property that PVC has which makes it suitable for covering electrical wires.

   _____

   _____

**10.** Argon is found in group 0 of the Periodic Table.

(a) Name the family of elements that argon belongs to.

_____

(b) The diagram represents an atom of argon.

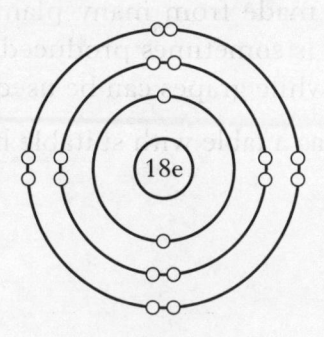

Label the structure **on the diagram** that represents the nucleus.

(c) The table below shows the densities and atomic numbers of the elements found in group 0.

| Atomic number | 2 | 10 | 18 | 36 | 54 | 86 |
|---|---|---|---|---|---|---|
| Density | 0.18 | 0.90 | 1.78 | 3.71 | 5.85 | 9.97 |

Describe what happens to the density as the atomic number increases.

_____

**11.** Alcohol is made using the following chemical reaction.

$$\text{glucose} \xrightarrow{\text{yeast}} \text{alcohol} + \text{carbon dioxide}$$

(a) What is the chemical name for alcohol?

_____

(b) (i) Alcoholic drinks can be made from many plants. Juniper berries are used to make gin. Vodka is sometimes produced from potatoes. Barley is used to make whiskey while grapes can be used to make wine.

Present this information as a table with suitable headings.

(ii) Whisky has a much higher concentration of alcohol than wine.

Name the process used to increase the alcohol concentration of drinks.

_____

(c) Sulphur dioxide is added to wine to stop bacteria attacking it.

Write the formula for sulphur dioxide.

_____

**12.** Batteries are used to produce electricity.

(a) Give **one** advantage of the use of a battery instead of mains electricity.

_____

_____

(b) After a while a battery needs to be replaced.

Explain why the battery stops producing electricity.

_____

_____

(c) A battery was made of 65% electrolyte and 12% carbon. The rest was made from other chemicals.

Label the pie chart to show the name and the percentage of each substance used to make this battery.

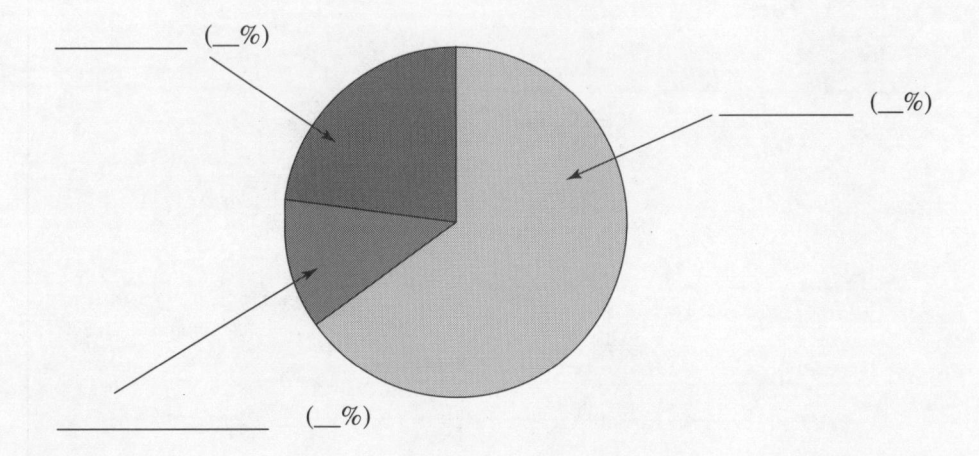

_____ (__%)

_____ (__%)

_____ (__%)

**13.** Compounds containing nitrogen and phosphorus are found in fertilisers.

(a) Many synthetic fertilisers are in increased use today.

(i) State what is meant by synthetic.

(ii) Phosphates are found in many fertilisers.

Suggest why zinc phosphate is **not** suitable as a fertiliser.

You may wish to use page 5 of the data booklet to help you.

(b) Pea plants contain bacteria that can convert nitrogen from the air into nitrogen compounds.

Where on the plant are the bacteria found?

**14.** A teacher split up lead bromide using the following apparatus.

*(a)* Name the type of experiment the teacher carried out.

*(b)* What would form at the negative electrode?

*(c)* Why do ionic compounds like lead bromide conduct electricity when molten?

*(d)* The electrodes are made from carbon (graphite).

Suggest a property of carbon that makes it suitable to be used as electrodes.

**15.** The following apparatus can be used to measure the volume of oxygen gas released when hydrogen peroxide decomposes.

*(a)* The manganese dioxide is a catalyst for the reaction.

What mass of catalyst is present once the reaction has ended?

_____ g

*(b)* State the test for oxygen gas.

_____

*(c)* The following graph shows the volume of oxygen produced during the reaction.

The reaction was carried out at 20 °C.

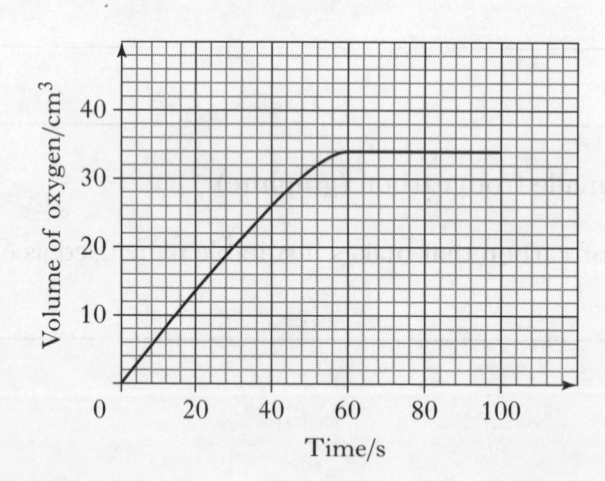

(i) What volume of oxygen was produced after 30 seconds?

_____ cm³

(ii) Sketch a line **on the graph** showing the result of carrying out the same experiment at 40°C.

**16.** The following experiments were carried out between some metals and dilute acid.

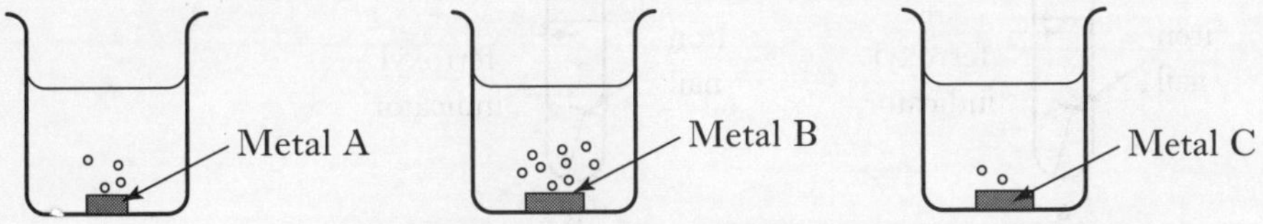

- Metal A
- Metal B
- Metal C

(a) Place the metals in order of reactivity (most reactive first)

_____

(b) The experiment was repeated using another metal but no bubbles were produced.

Suggest a name for this metal.

You can refer to page 7 of the data booklet to assist you.

_____

(c) Name the gas that is produced when the metals react with dilute acid.

_____

**17.** A pupil set up the following experiment to investigate rusting.

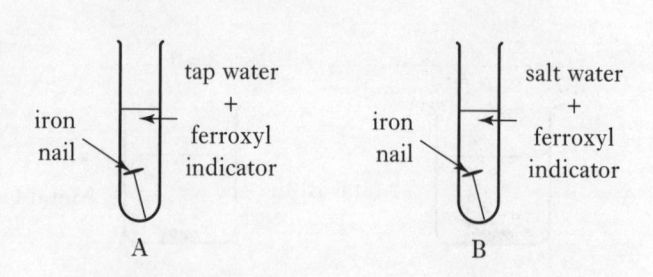

(a) (i) After a few minutes the indicator changes from yellow to blue.

Suggest a difference that would be seen between test tubes A and B.

_____

_____

(ii) Which ion turns ferroxyl indicator blue?

_____

(b) The pupil then set up two experiments to investigate how iron can be protected from rusting by sacrificial protection.

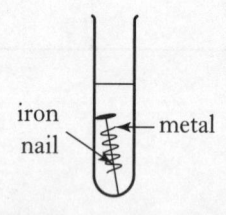

Suggest a metal that would be suitable to use in sacrificial protection.

You can refer to page 7 of the data booklet to assist you.

_____

**18.** The table below shows some uses of the gas butane.

| Uses of butane | % |
|---|---|
| bottled fuel | 35 |
| LPG fuel | 45 |
| lighter fuel | 8 |
| aerosol propellant | 10 |
| other | 2 |

(a) Using the graph paper below, create a bar chart that illustrates the information in the table.

*Remember to use appropriate scales when drawing the bar chart.*

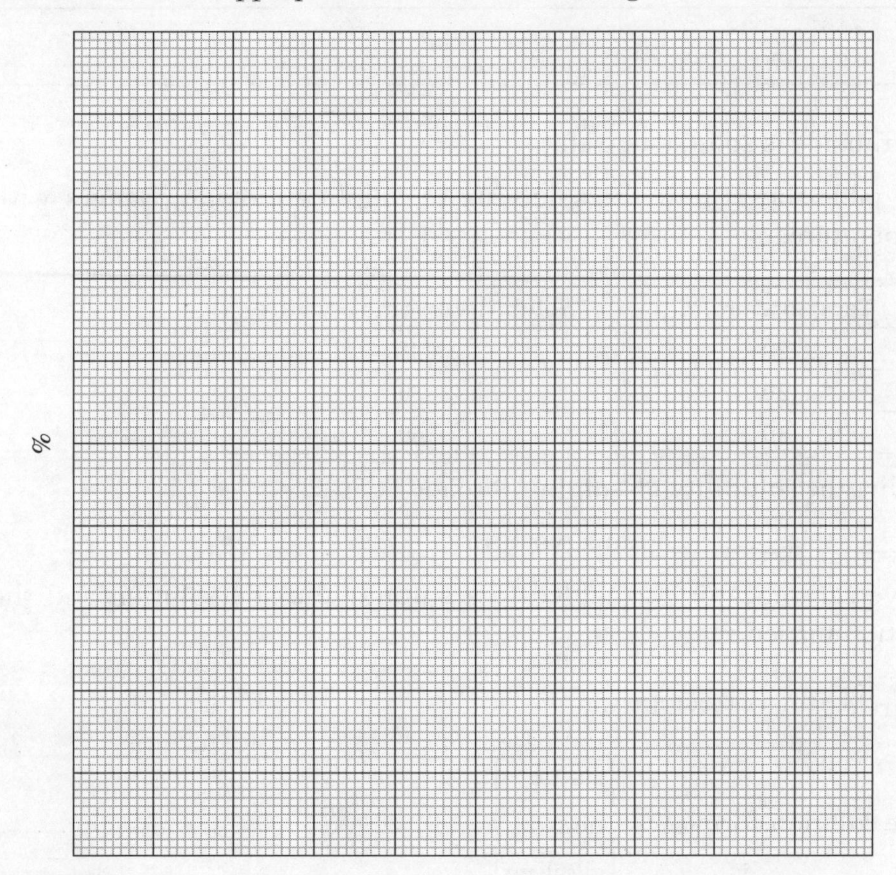

(b) One of the main uses of butane is as a fuel.

What is the meaning of the term fuel?

_____

(c) Butane can be made by reacting butene with hydrogen

butene + hydrogen → butane

(i) Name the **type** of reaction taking place.

_____

| KU | PS |
|---|---|

(ii) Draw the full structural formula of **butene.** — KU 1

**19.** Sulphur dioxide is a gas that pollutes the air.

(*a*) Suggest a source that can result in sulphur dioxide being present in the air.

________________________________________

________________________________________ — KU 1

(*b*) Sulphur dioxide is soluble in water.

(i) The table shows how the solubility of sulphur dioxide changes with temperature.

| Temperature/°C | Solubility/grams per litre |
|---|---|
| 20 | 110 |
| 30 | 80 |
| 40 | 60 |

Predict the solubility of sulphur dioxide at 50°C

__________________grams per litre — PS 1

(ii) Universal indicator was added to a sulphur dioxide solution and the solution turned red.

(Circle) the correct answer.

The solution formed is { acidic / neutral / alkaline } — PS 1

[End of Question Paper]

# Exam C

# Chemistry

## Standard Grade: General

Practice Papers
For SQA Exams

Exam C

**Fill in these boxes:**

Name of centre

Town

Forename(s)

Surname

You have 1 hour 30 minutes to complete this paper.

Try to answer all of the questions in the time allowed.

You will find data you need in the SQA Data Booklet.

You may answer questions in any order but you must write your answers in this book, in ink, and clearly label them.

Rough work should also be done in this book, but clearly crossed out.

Leckie×Leckie
Scotland's leading educational publishers

Practice Papers for SQA Exams: Standard Grade General Chemistry, Practice Exam C

## PART 1

**A total of 20 marks is available in this part of the paper.**

1. The names of some elements are shown below.

| A | B | C |
|---|---|---|
| lithium | oxygen | potassium |
| D | E | F |
| silver | zinc | sulphur |

(a) Identify the element with the lowest atomic number.

You can refer to page 8 of the data booklet to assist you.

| A | B | C |
|---|---|---|
| D | E | F |

(b) Identify the element that could be used to galvanise an iron gate.

| A | B | C |
|---|---|---|
| D | E | F |

(c) Identify the element that has the highest density.

You can refer to page 3 of the data booklet to assist you.

| A | B | C |
|---|---|---|
| D | E | F |

(d) Identify the **two** elements that combine to form a covalent compound.

| A | B | C |
|---|---|---|
| D | E | F |

Page 60

| KU | PS |
|---|---|

**2.** The names of some hydrocarbons are shown below.

| | | |
|---|---|---|
| A<br>octane | B<br>hexane | C<br>propene |
| D<br>pentene | E<br>ethene | F<br>butene |

(*a*) Identify the **two** alkanes.

| | | |
|---|---|---|
| A | B | C |
| D | E | F |

KU: 1

(*b*) Identify the hydrocarbon with a boiling point of −6°C.

You can refer to page 6 of the data booklet to assist you.

| | | |
|---|---|---|
| A | B | C |
| D | E | F |

PS: 1

(*c*) Identify the hydrocarbon that is the second member of the alkene family.

| | | |
|---|---|---|
| A | B | C |
| D | E | F |

KU: 1

**3.** The grid below shows the names of some compounds.

| A | B | C |
|---|---|---|
| magnesium bromide | lithium carbonate | sodium sulphite |
| D | E | F |
| calcium chloride | ammonium nitrate | calcium sulphite |

(a) Identify the **two** compounds that contain only two elements.

| A | B | C |
|---|---|---|
| D | E | F |

(b) Identify the compound that could be a useful fertiliser.

| A | B | C |
|---|---|---|
| D | E | F |

**4.** Julie tested the pH of various household substances.

Her results are shown in the table below.

|   | Household substance | pH |
|---|---|---|
| A | lime juice | 3 |
| B | vinegar | 4 |
| C | common salt | 7 |
| D | sugar | 7 |
| E | bicarbonate of soda | 9 |
| F | washing powder | 11 |

(a) Identify the **two** substances that will show an **increase** in pH when diluted.

| A | B | C |
|---|---|---|
| D | E | F |

(b) Identify the substance that is the most acidic.

| A | B | C |
|---|---|---|
| D | E | F |

5. The names of some chemical processes and reactions are shown below.

| A polymerisation | B electrolysis | C fermentation |
|---|---|---|
| D distillation | E photosynthesis | F respiration |

(a) Identify the reaction that requires chlorophyll.

| A | B | C |
|---|---|---|
| D | E | F |

(b) Identify the reaction that is used to make plastics.

| A | B | C |
|---|---|---|
| D | E | F |

(c) Identify the process that can be used to split up a compound into its elements.

| A | B | C |
|---|---|---|
| D | E | F |

6. The grid below shows some methods of protecting iron from rusting.

| A painting | B galvanising |
|---|---|
| C oiling/greasing | D coating with plastic |

Identify the most suitable method for protecting a bicycle chain.

| A | B |
|---|---|
| C | D |

7. Zinc and silver are both useful metals.

Identify the statement that is true for **both** zinc and silver.

You can refer to page 7 of the data booklet to assist you.

| A | They are found uncombined in the Earth's crust. |
|---|---|
| B | They react with water. |
| C | They can be used in the sacrificial protection of iron. |
| D | They are less reactive than magnesium. |
| E | They are stored under oil. |

**8.** Many substances exist as gases.

| A | B | C |
|---|---|---|
| carbon dioxide | hydrogen | nitrogen |
| D | E | F |
| oxygen | helium | carbon monoxide |

(a) Identify the gas that is poisonous.

| A | B | C |
|---|---|---|
| D | E | F |

(b) Identify the gas that is used up during respiration.

| A | B | C |
|---|---|---|
| D | E | F |

**9.** Andrew was asked to set up the following experiments.

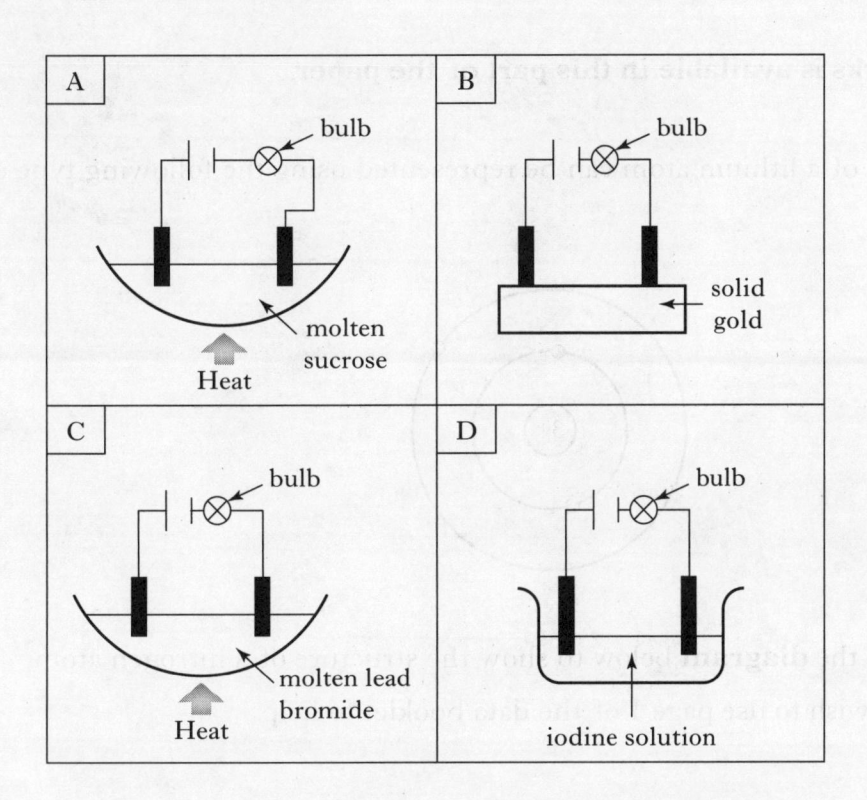

Identify the **two** experiments that would cause the bulb to go on.

| A | B |
|---|---|
| C | D |

PART 2

**A total of 40 marks is available in this part of the paper.**

10. The structure of a lithium atom can be represented using the following type of diagram.

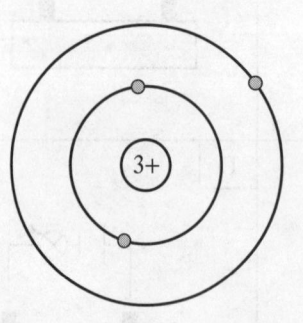

    (a) Complete the **diagram** below to show the structure of a nitrogen atom.

    You may wish to use page 1 of the data booklet to help.

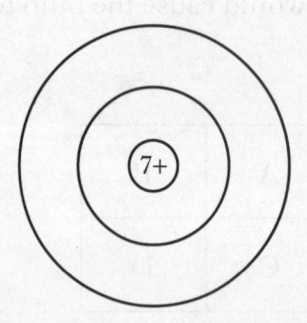

    (b) Lithium is found in group 1 of the Periodic Table.

    Name the family of elements to which it belongs.

    _____

**11.** Crude oil is separated by fractional distillation in a tower like the one shown below.

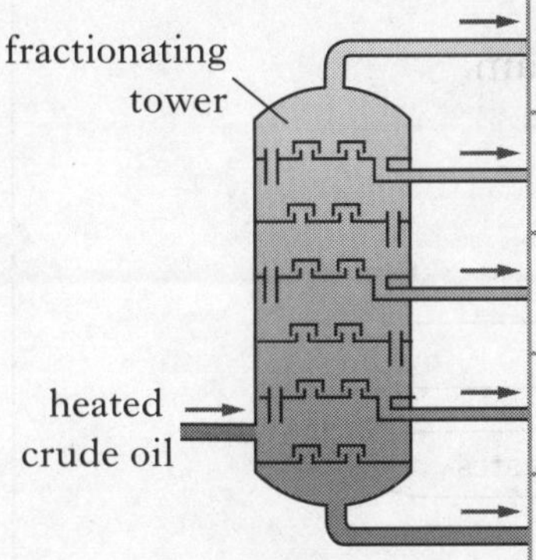

| Fraction | Temperature range (°C) | Number of carbon atoms per molecule |
|---|---|---|
| Refinery gas | <20 | 1–4 |
| Naphtha | 20–175 | 5–12 |
| Kerosene | 150–240 | 11–16 |
| Gas oil | 240–350 | 15–25 |
| Residue | >350 | >25 |

(a) The different fractions and their boiling ranges are shown.

   (i) The flammability of the fractions varies.

      Is kerosene or naphtha the more flammable fraction?

_____

   (ii) More people are choosing to travel by aeroplane now.

      From which fraction is aircraft fuel obtained?

_____

(b) Crude oil is a mixture of hydrocarbons.

   Name the elements present in a hydrocarbon.

_____

**12.** Extraction of Lead

Impure lead sulphide is roasted in an oven to produce lead oxide, sulphides and silicates. Carbon is then reacted with the lead oxide in a furnace to make impure lead and carbon dioxide. The impure lead can then undergo electrolysis to produce pure lead and impurities.

(a) Use the above information to complete the flow diagram.

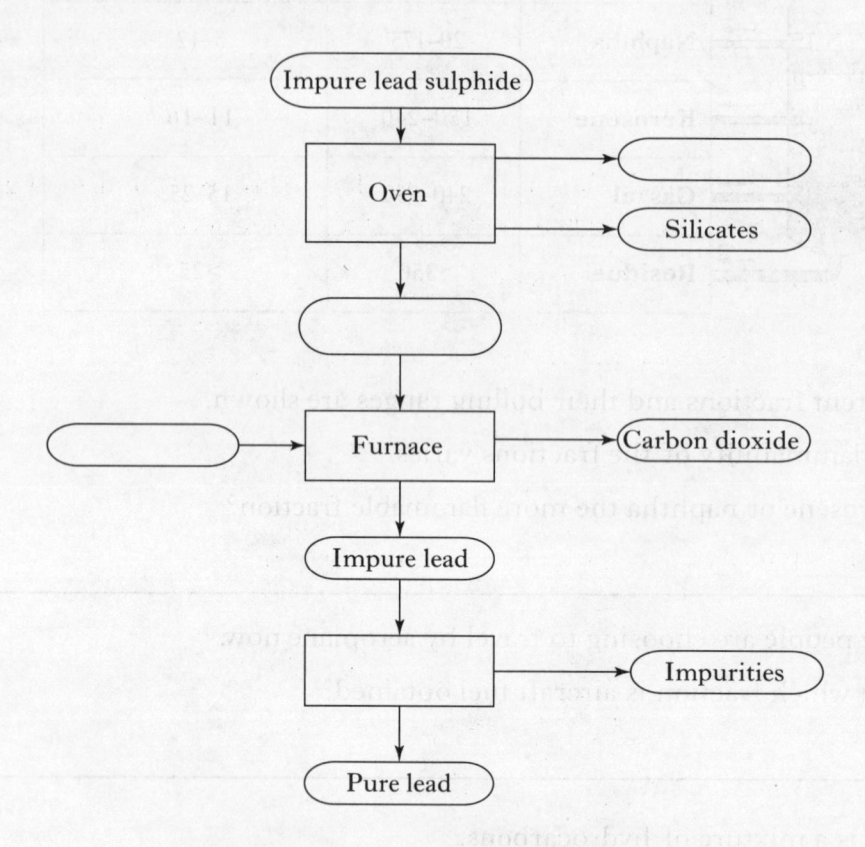

```
         Impure lead sulphide
                  │
                  ▼
               ┌──────┐  →  (         )
               │ Oven │
               └──────┘  →  ( Silicates )
                  │
                  ▼
              (         )
                  │
                  ▼
  (       ) → ┌─────────┐ → ( Carbon dioxide )
              │ Furnace │
              └─────────┘
                  │
                  ▼
             ( Impure lead )
                  │
                  ▼
              ┌─────────┐ → ( Impurities )
              │         │
              └─────────┘
                  │
                  ▼
             ( Pure lead )
```

(b) 8 million tonnes of lead were extracted worldwide in a year.

25% of this lead was extracted from recycled scrap metal.

How many tonnes of lead were extracted from recycled scrap metal?

_____ million tonnes

(c) Lead can be produced in the laboratory when lead oxide is heated strongly with carbon powder. The gas carbon dioxide is also produced.

Write a word equation for this reaction.

_____

(d) The lead-acid battery is used to make a rechargeable battery.

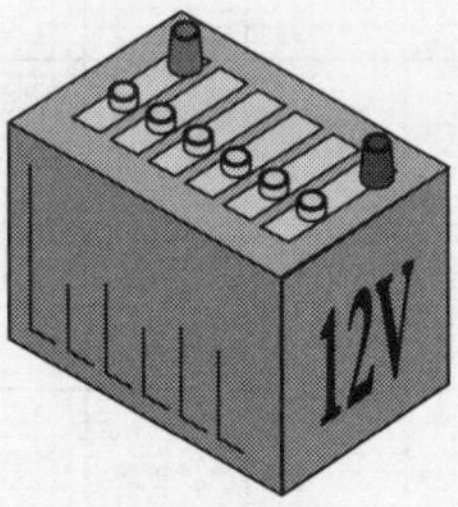

The acid acts as an electrolyte.

What is the purpose of the electrolyte?

_____

**13.** The ion content of a sample of sea water is shown in the pie chart below.

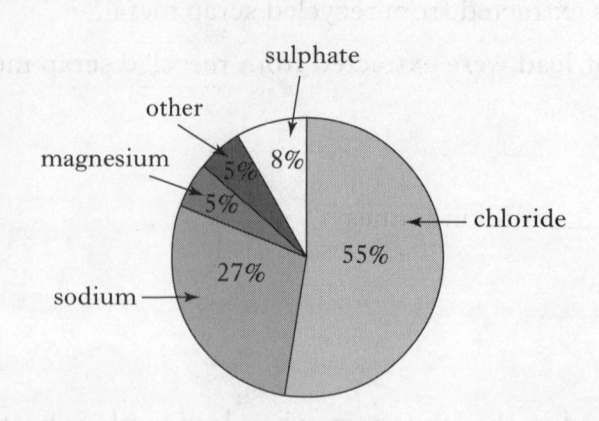

- sulphate 8%
- other 5%
- magnesium 5%
- sodium 27%
- chloride 55%

(a) Using the graph paper below, create a bar chart that illustrates the information in the table.

*Remember to use appropriate scales when drawing the bar chart.*

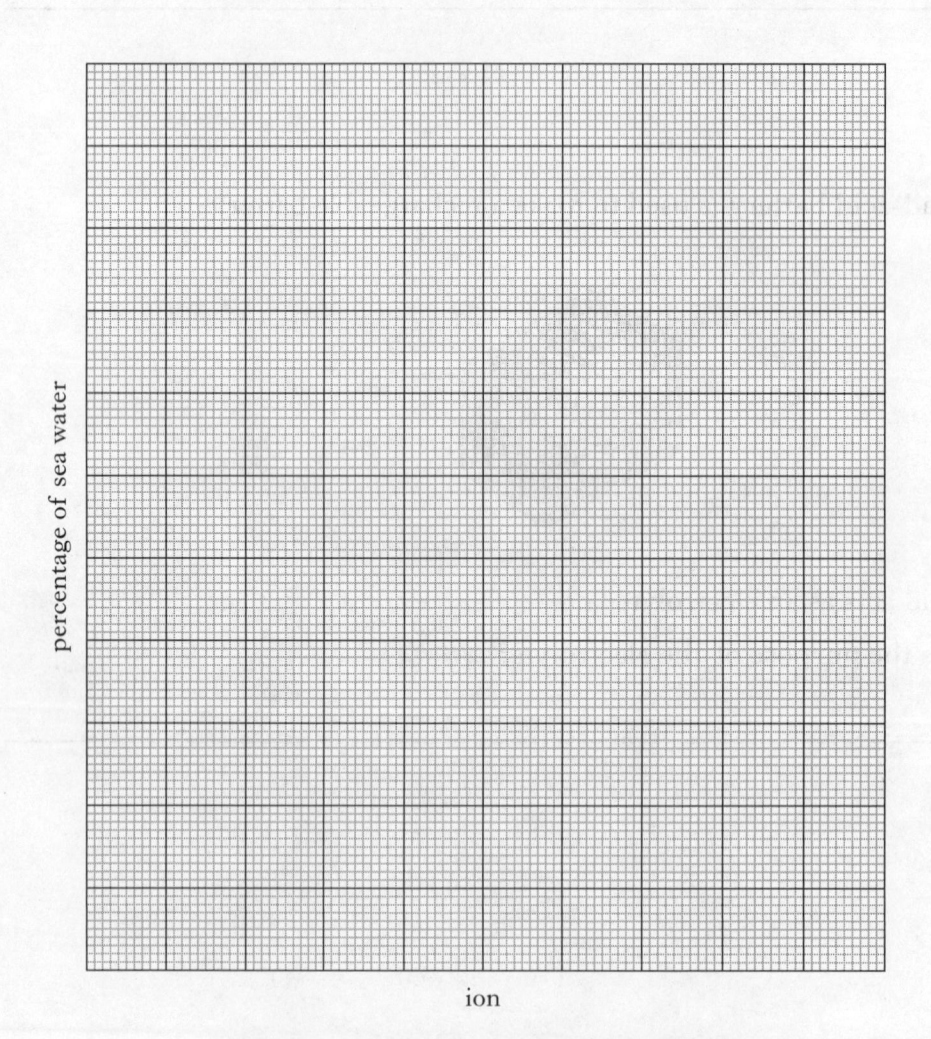

percentage of sea water

ion

(b) The compound magnesium sulphate is found in sea water.
Write the formula for magnesium sulphate.

14. The table below shows some materials made by mixing different metals.

| Name of material | Metals it is made from |
|---|---|
| duralumin | copper |
| | aluminium |
| | magnesium |
| | manganese |
| aluminium bronze | copper |
| | aluminium |

(a) What term should be used to describe a mixture of metals?

_____

(b) The material duralumin is used to make aircraft bodywork.

One reason duralumin is used to make aircraft bodywork is because it is very strong.

Give **another** property of duralumin that would make it suitable to make aircraft bodywork.

_____

_____

(c) The strength of a piece of aluminium bronze depends on the percentage of aluminium it contains.

| % of aluminium in aluminium bronze | Strength of aluminium bronze/units |
|---|---|
| 2 | 121 |
| 4 | 144 |
| 6 | 169 |
| 8 | 187 |

Predict the relative strength of aluminium bronze that contains 10% aluminium.

_____ units

15. There are many different compounds of sulphur.

(a) Zinc sulphate can be dissolved in water.

Circle the correct answer.

Zinc sulphate can be called the { solute / solvent / solution }

(b) Zinc sulphate solution was mixed with solution X to form insoluble zinc carbonate.

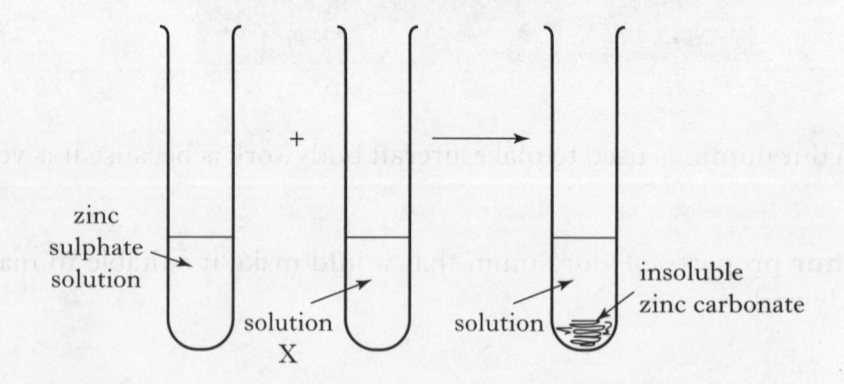

(i) Suggest a name for solution X.

You can refer to page 5 of the data booklet to assist you.

_____

(ii) How could the insoluble zinc carbonate be separated from the solution?

_____

_____

(c) Sulphur can react with metals to form sulphides.

The solubility of some sulphides is shown below.

| Sulphide | Solubility |
| --- | --- |
| potassium sulphide | very soluble |
| zinc sulphide | insoluble |
| lithium sulphide | very soluble |
| copper sulphide | insoluble |
| silver sulphide | insoluble |

What general rule can be made about the **transition metal** sulphides?

You can refer to page 8 of the data booklet to assist you.

_____

_____

1

**16.** There are many different plastics.

(a) Plastics used to make plugs do **not** soften on heating.

What term is used to describe plastics with this property?

_____

1

(b) Most plastics are non-biodegradable.

Suggest a reason why this can be an advantage.

_____

_____

1

(c) Vinylchloride is a monomer used to make a plastic.

Name the plastic made from vinylchloride.

_____

1

| KU | PS |
|---|---|

**17.** Isla investigated a reaction involving copper carbonate and acid using the apparatus below.

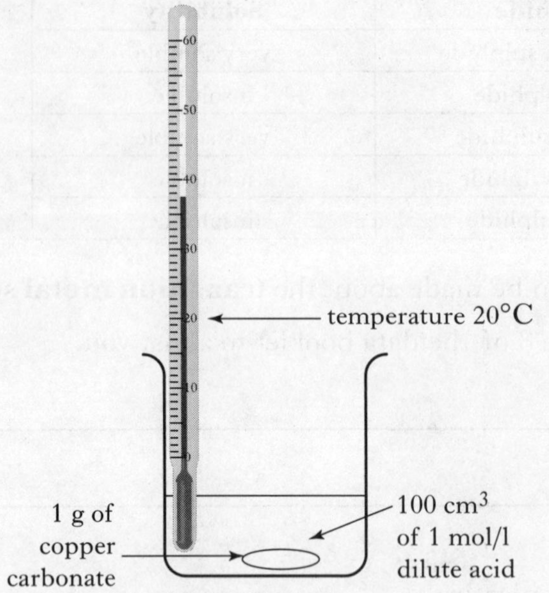

60
50
40
30
20
10
0
temperature 20°C
1 g of
copper
carbonate
100 cm³
of 1 mol/l
dilute acid


(*a*) When copper carbonate is added to dilute acid, the products are a salt, water and carbon dioxide.

(i) Name this type of reaction.

______________________________ 1

(ii) State the test for carbon dioxide gas.

______________________________

______________________________ 1

(b) Isla wanted to see if raising the temperature to 40°C would speed up the reaction.

Complete the diagram to show how she would make her second experiment a fair test.

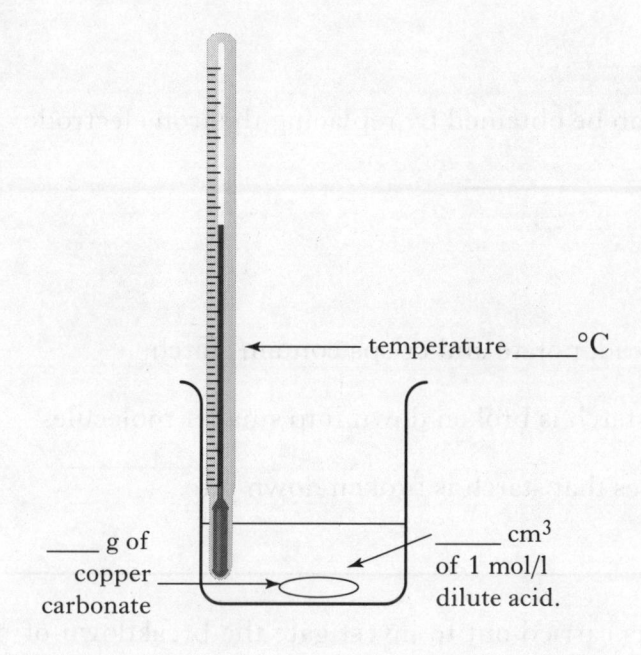

____ g of copper carbonate

temperature ____ °C

____ cm³ of 1 mol/l dilute acid.

**18.** A cell can be made by connecting two different metals in solutions of their ions.

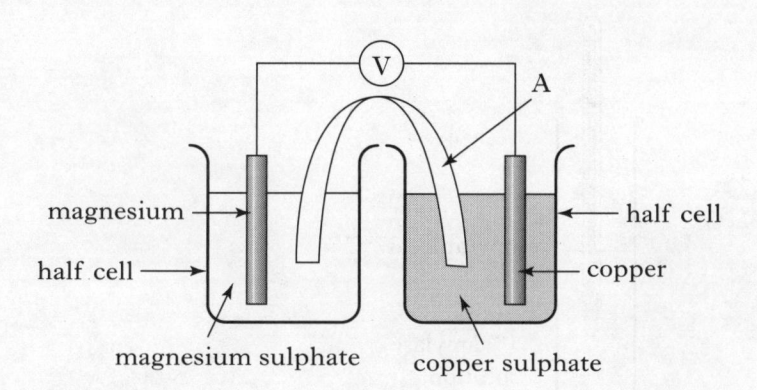

magnesium half cell — magnesium sulphate
half cell — copper
copper sulphate

(a) Name the piece of apparatus A which is used to complete the circuit.

_____

(b) Draw an arrow **on the diagram** to show the direction of electron flow.

(c) If iron was replaced with another metal, the voltage would change.

Circle the correct answer

You can refer to page 7 of the data booklet to assist you.

A higher voltage can be obtained by replacing the iron electrode with $\begin{Bmatrix} \text{zinc} \\ \text{silver} \end{Bmatrix}$

19. Many foods such as bread, potato and crisps contain starch.

(a) During digestion starch is broken down into smaller molecules.

Name the molecules that starch is broken down into.

_____

(b) An experiment was carried out to investigate the breakdown of starch in a piece of bread.

A biological catalyst called amylase was used.

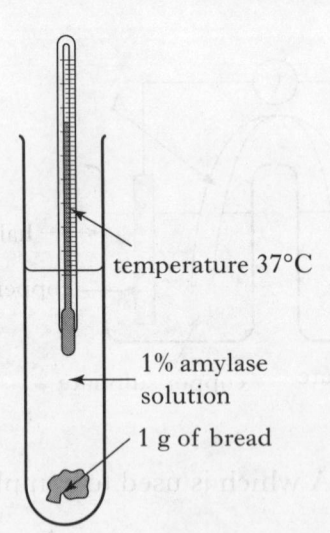

- temperature 37°C
- 1% amylase solution
- 1 g of bread

(i) What name is given to describe a biological catalyst like amylase?

_____

(ii) During the experiment a sample was taken from the test tube every five minutes and added to iodine solution.

Describe what you would expect to see happen to the iodine if the starch had not yet broken down.

_____

_____

(iii) The experiment was repeated using 1g of **smaller** bread pieces.

What effect would using smaller bread pieces have on the rate of starch breakdown?

_____

20. Nitrogen dioxide can be made by the sparking of air.

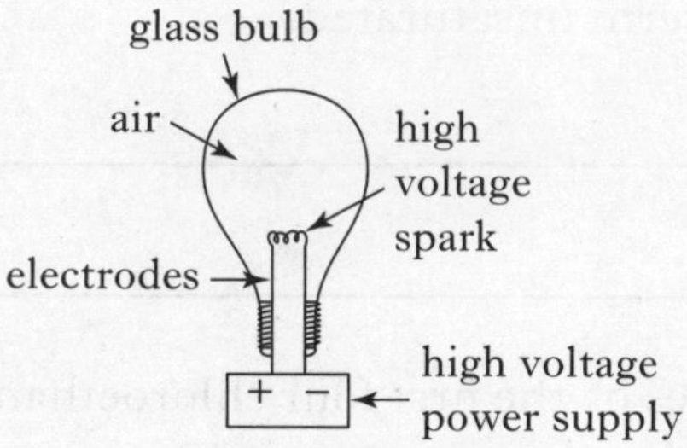

(a) Nitrogen and oxygen in the air combine to form nitrogen dioxide.

(i) Explain why a high voltage spark is needed.

_____

_____

(ii) Once the nitrogen dioxide had formed, damp pH paper was added to the flask.

Describe the effect nitrogen dioxide would have on damp pH paper.

_____

_____

(b) Air is a mixture of the **diatomic** gases nitrogen and oxygen.

What is meant by the term diatomic?

_____

_____

Practice Papers for SQA Exams: Standard Grade General Chemistry, Practice Exam C

**21.** Ethene can be used to make the compounds known as the chloroethanes.

(a) To make monochloroethane the following reaction is used:

$$\text{ethene + hydrogen} \xrightarrow{\text{catalyst}} \text{monochloroethane}$$

(i) Why is a catalyst used?

_____

_____

1

(ii) Ethene is an **unsaturated** hydrocarbon.

What is meant by the term unsaturated?

_____

_____

1

(b) The names and/or structures of the first four chloroethanes are shown in the table.

| Name | Molecular formula | Full structural Formula |
|---|---|---|
| monochloroethane | $C_2H_5Cl$ | 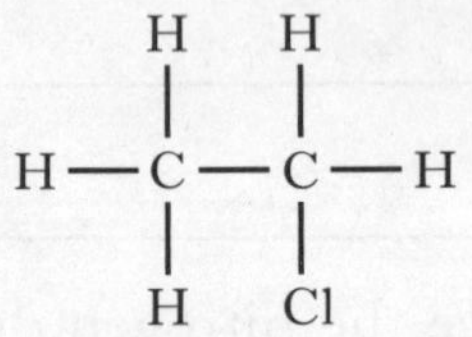 H-C(H)(H)-C(H)(H)-Cl (H H above, H Cl below) |
| dichloroethane | $C_2H_4Cl_2$ | 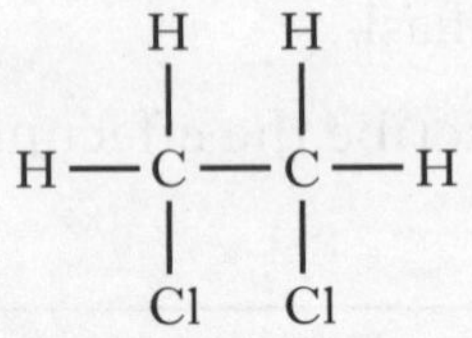 H-C(H)(Cl)-C(H)(Cl)-H |
| trichloroethane | $C_2H_3Cl_3$ | |
| | $C_2H_2Cl_4$ | 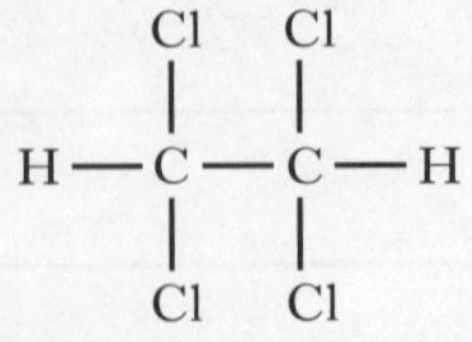 H-C(Cl)(Cl)-C(Cl)(Cl)-H |

(i) Draw the full structural formula for trichloroethane.

1

Page 80

(ii) Name the compound with the formula $C_2H_2Cl_4$

_____

[End of Question Paper]

Exam D

# Chemistry   Standard Grade: General

Practice Papers  
For SQA Exams

Exam D

**Fill in these boxes:**

Name of centre

Town

Forename(s)

Surname

You have 1 hour 30 minutes to complete this paper.

Try to answer all of the questions in the time allowed.

You will find data you need in the SQA Data Booklet.

You may answer questions in any order but you must write your answers in this book, in ink, and clearly label them.

Rough work should also be done in this book, but clearly crossed out.

**Leckie × Leckie**
Scotland's leading educational publishers

# PART 1

**A total of 20 marks is available in this part of the paper.**

1. The simplest substances are the elements.

   | A hydrogen | B nitrogen | C oxygen |
   |---|---|---|
   | D silver | E fluorine | F iron |

   (a) Identify the element that is a halogen.

   You can refer to page 6 of the data booklet to assist you.

   | A | B | C |
   |---|---|---|
   | D | E | F |

   (b) Identify the element that makes up about 80% of the air.

   | A | B | C |
   |---|---|---|
   | D | E | F |

   (c) Identify the element that has the lowest melting point.

   You can refer to page 3 of the data booklet to assist you.

   | A | B | C |
   |---|---|---|
   | D | E | F |

   (d) Identify the element that can be found uncombined in the Earth's crust.

   | A | B | C |
   |---|---|---|
   | D | E | F |

2. Rhona was investigating how quickly an indigestion tablet reacted.

The acid used in each experiment was the same concentration and volume.

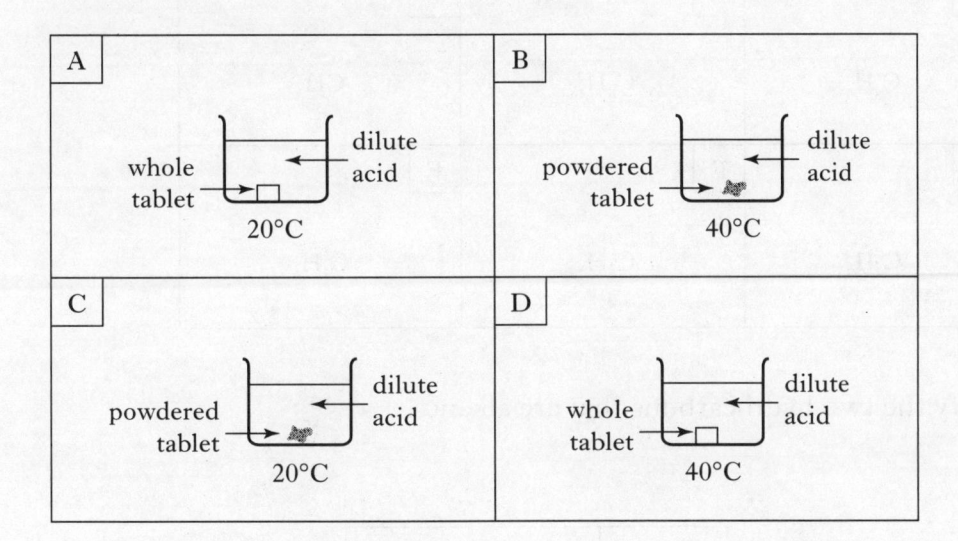

| A — whole tablet, dilute acid, 20°C | B — powdered tablet, dilute acid, 40°C |
| C — powdered tablet, dilute acid, 20°C | D — whole tablet, dilute acid, 40°C |

In which experiment would the indigestion tablet react the quickest?

| A | B |
| C | D |

3. The grid below contains the molecular formulae for some hydrocarbons.

| A $C_3H_6$ | B $C_6H_{14}$ | C $CH_4$ |
|---|---|---|
| D $C_4H_8$ | E $C_6H_{12}$ | F $C_2H_4$ |

(a) Identify the **two** hydrocarbons that are alkanes.

| A | B | C |
|---|---|---|
| D | E | F |

(b) Identify the molecular formula for propene.

| A | B | C |
|---|---|---|
| D | E | F |

4. Part of the Periodic Table is shown below.

The letters do **not** represent the symbols for the elements.

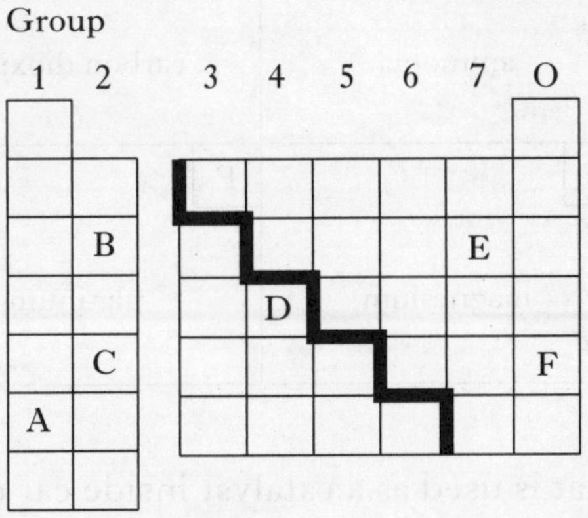

Group
1 2 3 4 5 6 7 0

(positions: B in group 2, C in group 2, A in group 1; D in group 4, E in group 6, F in group 0)

(a) Identify the **two** elements with similar chemical properties.

| A | B | C |
|---|---|---|
| D | E | F |

(b) Identify the alkali metal.

| A | B | C |
|---|---|---|
| D | E | F |

(c) Identify the element with the electron arrangement 2,8,2.

You can refer to page 1 of the data booklet to assist you.

| A | B | C |
|---|---|---|
| D | E | F |

**5.** The grid shows the names of some substances.

| A | B | C |
|---|---|---|
| crude oil | ammonia | carbon dioxide |
| D | E | F |
| oxygen | magnesium | platinum |

(a) Identify the substance that is used as a catalyst inside car exhaust systems.

| A | B | C |
|---|---|---|
| D | E | F |

(b) Identify the mixture.

| A | B | C |
|---|---|---|
| D | E | F |

(c) Identify the substance that is used to make fertilisers.

| A | B | C |
|---|---|---|
| D | E | F |

**6.** The grid shows the name of some oxides.

| A<br>lithium oxide | B<br>iron oxide | C<br>sulphur dioxide |
|---|---|---|
| D<br>magnesium oxide | E<br>nitrogen dioxide | F<br>potassium oxide |

(a) Identify the **two** oxides that would form an acidic solution when dissolved in water.

(b) Identify the oxide that is used in the blast furnace.

(c) Identify the oxide made during lightning storms.

**7.** Electrochemical cells are used to produce electricity

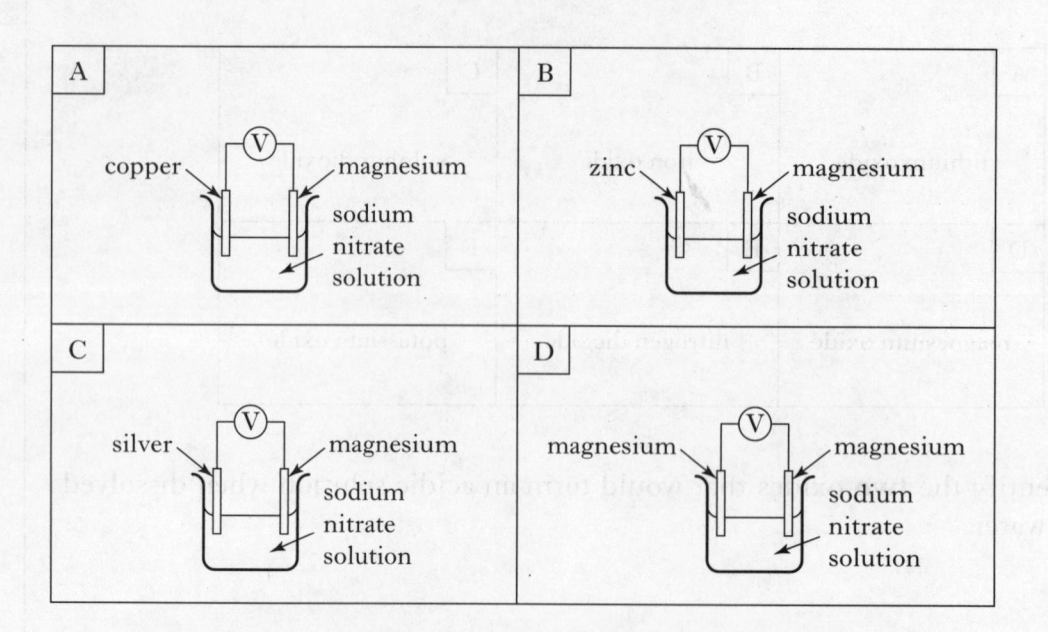

| | |
|---|---|
| **A** copper — magnesium, sodium nitrate solution | **B** zinc — magnesium, sodium nitrate solution |
| **C** silver — magnesium, sodium nitrate solution | **D** magnesium — magnesium, sodium nitrate solution |

(a) Which arrangement gives the largest reading on the voltmeter?

You can refer to page 7 of the data booklet to assist you.

| A | B |
|---|---|
| C | D |

(b) Identify which arrangement would **not** produce electricity.

| A | B |
|---|---|
| C | D |

8. Glucose and sucrose are substances found in many foods.

   Identify the **two** statements that are true for both glucose and sucrose.

   | A | They are hydrocarbons. |
   |---|---|
   | B | They burn to produce carbon dioxide and water. |
   | C | They are made during photosynthesis. |
   | D | They turn Benedict's solution from blue to orange. |
   | E | They contain the elements carbon, hydrogen and oxygen. |

   PS: 2

## PART 2

**A total of 40 marks is available in this part of the paper.**

9. Most plastics and synthetic fibres are made from chemicals found in crude oil.

    (a) Nylon is a synthetic fibre that has many properties and uses. Nylon climbing ropes are very strong. Shirts made from nylon are quick drying. Carpets can be made from nylon and are hard wearing. Many tennis racquet strings are nylon as they are flexible.

    Present the information above in a table with two headings.

    (b) Describe the formation of crude oil

    _____

    _____

    _____

    (c) Very few plastics and synthetic fibres are biodegradable.

    What is meant by 'biodegradable'?

    _____

    _____

10. The cracking of paraffin into smaller hydrocarbons can be carried out in the laboratory.

(a) Some of the products of cracking are unsaturated.

**Complete the diagram** to show how the presence of unsaturated hydrocarbons could be tested for.

(b) One of the reactions taking place is:

alkane A → C$_5$H$_{12}$ + C$_2$H$_4$
          pentane    ethene

(i) Draw the full structural formula for pentane.

(ii) Write the molecular formula for alkane A.

(c) Ethene is a molecule produced in cracking which can be converted into poly(ethene) by polymerisation.

Draw how the ethene molecules could join together to form a section of poly(ethene)

**11.** The table below shows three chemical reactions carried out in the laboratory.

| Reaction | Description of reaction |
|---|---|
| 1 | glucose was broken down into alcohol and carbon dioxide using yeast |
| 2 | mercury oxide was heated strongly and broken down into its elements. |
| 3 | magnesium was burned in oxygen to produce magnesium oxide |

(a) The following statement was made by a pupil.

Circle the correct word to complete the sentence.

The number of new substances produced in a chemical reaction is at least $\begin{Bmatrix} one \\ two \end{Bmatrix}$

(b) Reaction 1 is used by the drinks industry to make alcohol.

(i) Name this type of reaction.

_____

(ii) Carbon dioxide is also produced in this reaction.

Name the **type** of bonding found in carbon dioxide.

_____

(c) Write a word equation for reaction 2.

_____

**12.** **Production of hydrochloric acid**

Salt solution is split up using electrolysis. The products are chlorine, sodium hydroxide and hydrogen. The chlorine and hydrogen are re-combined in a hydrogen chloride oven. Hydrogen chloride enters an absorber where it is dissolved in water to produce hydrochloric acid.

(a) Use this information to complete the flow diagram.

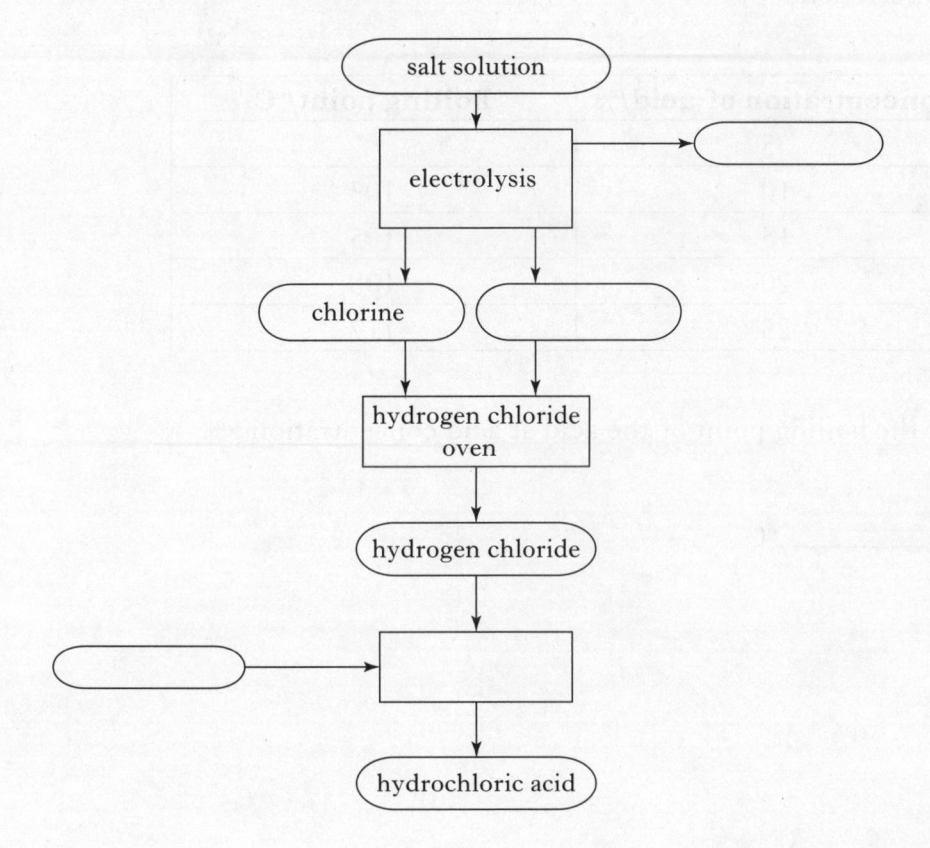

(b) Hydrochloric acid reacts with potassium oxide as shown.

potassium oxide + hydrochloric acid → a salt + water

Name the salt produced.

_____

(c) The boiling point of hydrochloric acid varies with the concentration of hydrochloric acid.

| Concentration of acid/% | Boiling point/°C |
|---|---|
| 5 | |
| 10 | 103 |
| 15 | 105 |
| 20 | 108 |
| 25 | 117 |

Predict the boiling point of the acid at acid concentration 5%

_____ °C

**13.** A chemistry teacher demonstrated the reaction of calcium with water and collected the gas made.

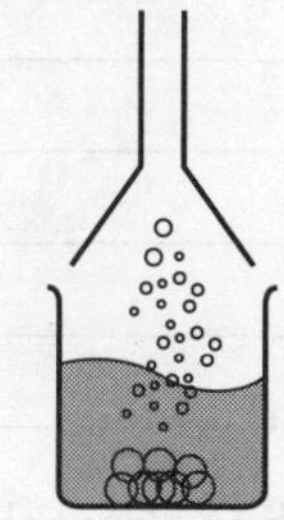

(a) The gas produced burns with a pop.

Name this gas.

_____

(b) An alkaline solution is produced when the metal reacts with water.

 (i) Describe how universal indicator or pH paper could be used to measure the pH of this solution.

_____

_____

 (ii) Name the **ion** that is found in all alkaline solutions.

_____

(c) If a substance has a density less than 1.00 g/cm³ it will float on water.

If a substance has density greater than 1.00 g/cm³ it will sink in water.

Will calcium sink or float on water?

You may wish to use page 2 of the SQA data booklet to help you.

_____

**14.** The table below shows the uses of zinc.

| Uses of zinc | % |
|---|---|
| galvanising | 56 |
| brass | 18 |
| batteries | 3 |
| chemicals | 22 |
| other uses | 1 |

(a) Using the graph paper below, create a bar chart that illustrates the information in the table.

*Remember to use appropriate scales when drawing the bar chart.*

(b) Iron can be protected from rusting by galvanising. This is when a layer of zinc covers the iron.

(i) How does the layer of zinc prevent rusting?

_____

_____

(ii) There are several methods to prevent iron from rusting.

Suggest one **other** method of protecting iron from rusting.

_____

(c) A sample of brass contained 78% zinc, 2% manganese and the rest was copper.

Label the pie chart to show the name and percentage for each part of the brass

_____ (____%)

_____ (____%)

_____ (____%)

**15.** The Ostwald process is an industrial process used to make nitric acid.

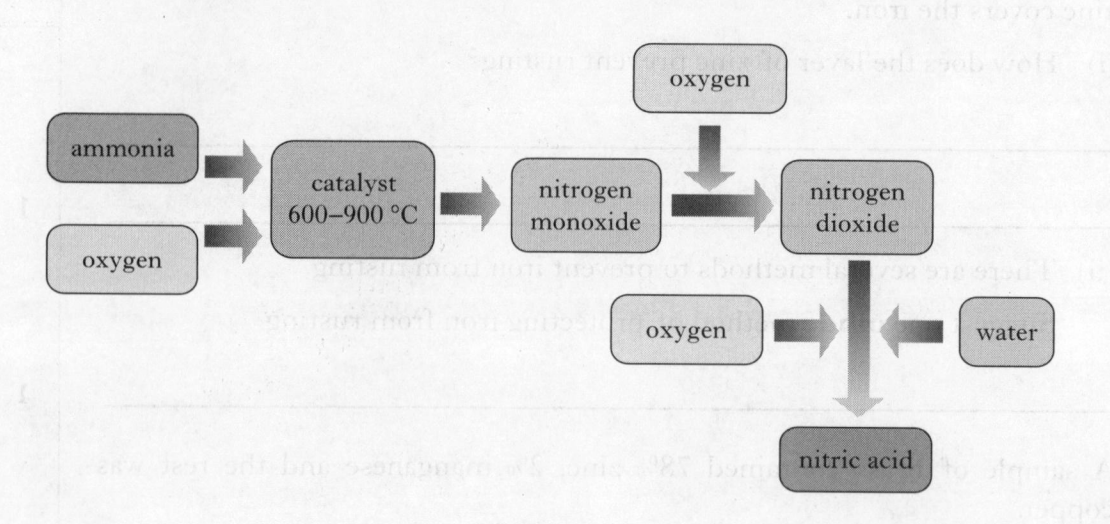

*(a)* (i) Name the catalyst used in the Ostwald process.

___

(ii) Nitrogen monoxide reacts with oxygen to produce nitrogen monoxide. Write the formula for nitrogen monoxide.

___

*(b)* Rainwater sometimes contains nitrates.

Suggest an advantage of rainwater that contains nitrates being absorbed by the soil.

___

**16.** Indigestion tablets and dental products contain many chemical compounds.

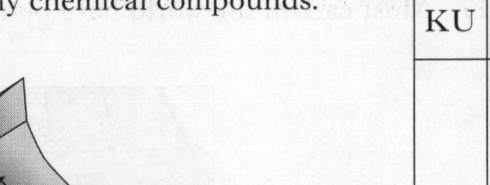

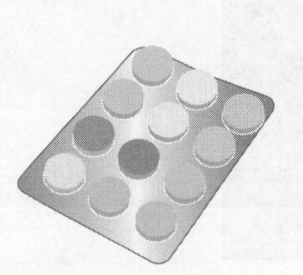

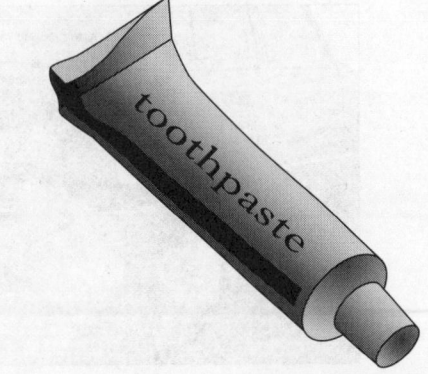

(a) (i) Excess acid in the stomach is neutralised when an indigestion tablet is taken.

Describe what happens to the pH of the stomach acid when the tablet is taken.

_____

_____

(ii) Some indigestion tablets contain calcium carbonate.

Name the gas produced when calcium carbonate reacts with acid.

_____

(b) Xylitol is a chemical compound found in some toothpastes.

The diagram shows a molecule of xylitol.

Complete the molecular formula for xylitol to showing the number of each type of atom in this molecule.

# C    H    O

**17.** Most cars in the world have petrol engines.

(a) Petrol is obtained from a crude oil fraction.

Name the process used to separate crude oil into its fractions.

_____

1

(b) A car oil was tested to find out how changing its temperature affected it.

The time taken for the oil to pass through a piece of glass tubing was measured.

The experiment was repeated with oil at different temperatures.

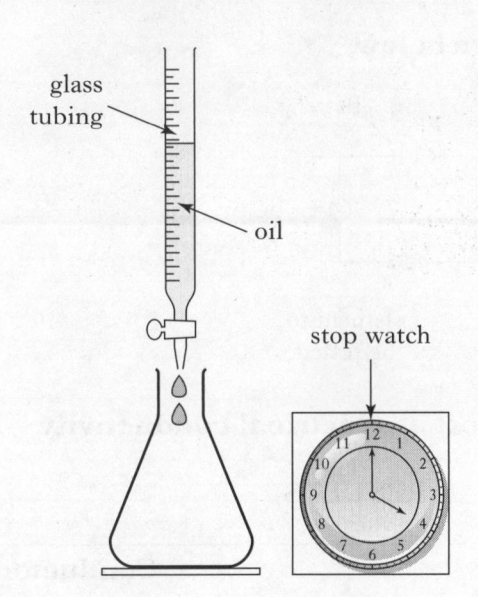

The results are shown below.

| Temperature of oil/°C | Time taken for oil to pass through the tube/s |
|---|---|
| 20 | 91 |
| 35 | 64 |
| 44 | 35 |
| 53 | 19 |

(i) What is the effect of increasing the temperature on the time taken for the oil to pass through the tubing.

(ii) Suggest a factor that should have been kept the same in each experiment to ensure a fair comparison between temperatures.

| KU | PS |
|---|---|

**18.** A student carried out an experiment to find out whether certain elements conducted electricity.

**WORKCARD**

**1. Set up the circuit shown below.**

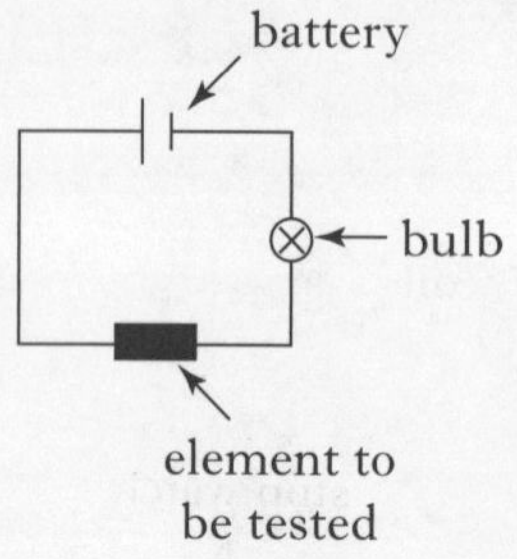


**2. Take an element and test its electrical conductivity.**

**RESULTS**

| Element | Metal or non-metal | Conductor of electricity |
|---|---|---|
| magnesium | metal | conductor |
| sulphur | non-metal | non-conductor |
| phosphorus | | |

(*a*) How would the pupil know if the element was a conductor of electricity?

_______________________________________________ 1 (PS)

(*b*) Name the particles that flow through the metal wires when conduction happens.

_______________________________________________ 1 (KU)

(*c*) Complete the above table to show the result the student would obtain if he used phosphorus.

You can refer to page 1 of the data booklet to assist you. 1 (PS)

(*d*) The experiment was repeated using some ionic compounds.

Explain why the **solid** ionic compounds did not conduct.

_______________________________________________

_______________________________________________ 1 (KU)

[End of Question Paper]

Worked Answers

# PRACTICE EXAM A — WORKED ANSWERS

## Part 1 – Grid Questions

> ★ 1. This question covers commonly asked questions on the elements of the Periodic Table. This type of question is usually the first question in a general paper. Notice that parts (a) and (d) guide you to the Periodic Table in the data booklet. You will be given a data booklet in the exam.

1. (a) E — **1 mark**
   (b) C — **1 mark**

   > **HINT:** Oxygen and water are required for rusting.

   **TOP EXAM TIP**
   Grid questions only have one answer, unless stated otherwise in the question.
   No half marks are given for the grid questions in Part 1 of the exam paper.

   (c) B — **1 mark**

   > **HINT:** The very unreactive non-metals are the noble gases. These are found in group 0 of the Periodic Table.

   (d) C — **1 mark**

   > **HINT:** On page eight of the data booklet, the date of discovery is the number underneath the symbol for the element.

   **TOP EXAM TIP**
   On page 8 of the data booklet is a key showing what the information in each box on the Periodic Table means.

> ★ 2. You should expect to answer a grid question on hydrocarbons, so make sure you know about them! Since 2004 a hydrocarbon grid has appeared in most exam papers.

   (a) D — **1 mark**

   > **HINT:** The **but-** part of **but**ene tells you that there are four carbons. You need to learn the first eight prefixes and the numbers they represent.
   >
   > You can learn prefixes by using a memory aid such as:
   >
   > | My | meth | 1 |
   > | Exam | eth | 2 |
   > | Paper | prop | 3 |
   > | Book | but | 4 |
   > | Provides | pent | 5 |
   > | Helpful | hex | 6 |
   > | Hints | hep | 7 |
   > | Often | oct | 8 |
   >
   > It is often better to come up with your own memory aid as you are more likely to remember it.

   **TOP EXAM TIP**
   You can write any kind of memory aids, working, etc. on the exam paper, if you find that helpful. Just make sure your final answer is clear.

*Page 109*

Worked Answers to Practice Exam A: General Chemistry

(b)  A    1 mark

> **HINT**  When looking up a boiling point or melting point on page 6 of the data booklet take care. For example, it could be easy to mix up eth**ane** with eth**ene**. Also make sure you don't get the melting points and boiling points mixed up.

| A | B | C |
|---|---|---|
| ethene | propane | pentene |
| −104°C | −40°C | 33°C |
| D | E | F |
| butane | ethane | hexane |
| −1°C | −89°C | 69°C |

**TOP EXAM TIP**

Make sure you know what information is in the data booklet. Page 6 contains some information for Standard Grade candidates and some for use by Intermediate 2 candidates. Make sure you know what information is for Standard Grade candidates.

(c)  A and C    1 mark

> **HINT**  When asked to identify an alk**ene** look for the name ending -**ene**.

**TOP EXAM TIP**

In a grid question when asked to look up data in the data booklet, it is useful to write the data down on the question paper. For example when asked to look up a boiling point, write the substances' boiling point in its box on the grid as you go along. This will help you to compare the boiling points and not get mixed up.

★ 3. This problem-solving question covers the concept of a fair test. This type of question is common in the exam. You need to compare the variables in each box.

(d)  D and E    1 mark.

> **HINT**  The question asks you for two experiments that show the effect of temperature on reaction rates, so you must pick two experiments which have different temperatures. The experiment has to be fair so **every other variable in the two experiments must be kept the same**. Therefore, in this example D and E are the correct answers as they have different temperatures (40°C and 20°C), but the same particle size (lumps) and same concentration of acid (1 mol/l).

**TOP EXAM TIP**

The 'rate of reaction' is the speed of reaction. The units mol/l are the units for concentration.

*Page 110*

# Worked Answers to Practice Exam A: General Chemistry

> ★ **4.** Simple diagrams are often used to represent different substances. You must know the meanings of element, compound and mixture to answer this question successfully.

(a) B and F  **1 mark**

> **HINT**
> An element is made from one type of atom. A compound is made from two or more different elements joined together. A mixture is formed when two substances are mixed together, not chemically joined.
>
> Look at each box in turn.
>
> Box A contains two different types of atoms, but they are **not** joined together so this represents a mixture of elements.
>
> Box B contains two different types of atoms, joined together so this represents a compound.
>
> Box C contains one type of atom so represents an element.
>
> Box D contains atoms joined together but they are the same type so this represents an element.
>
> Box E contains atoms joined together but they are the same type so this represents an element.
>
> Box F contains two different types of atoms, joined together so this represents a compound.

(b) D  **1 mark**

> **HINT**
> A **di**atomic molecule is made from **two** atoms joined together. The atoms can be same type or different. In this case they are the same type.

> ★ **5.** Three parts of this question test your knowledge of gases that are either used up or produced during reactions. There is also a gas test question. There is usually at least one gas test question in the exam.

> **HINT**
> The four gas tests you need to know are:
> 1. Oxygen relights a glowing splint.
> 2. Hydrogen burns with a pop.
> 3. Carbon dioxide turns limewater cloudy/milky.
> 4. Ammonia turns damp pH paper blue.

(a) D  **1 mark**

(b) E  **1 mark**

**TOP EXAM TIP**
Make sure you learn the four gas tests.

> **HINT**
> The name metal **carbon**ate suggests that the answer involves a carbon-containing gas. It is useful to learn the general word equation:
> metal carbonate + acid → a salt + water + carbon dioxide.

(c) D  **1 mark**

> **HINT**
> Learn the word equation for photosynthesis and you can answer this question:
> carbon dioxide + water → glucose + oxygen

## Worked Answers to Practice Exam A: General Chemistry

(d) B  1 mark

**HINT:** When a hydrocarbon is burned in a good supply of oxygen/air, carbon dioxide and water are produced. During **incomplete** combustion of a hydrocarbon, there is not enough oxygen present so carbon monoxide will be formed instead of carbon dioxide.

**TOP EXAM TIP:** Remember you can write anywhere on the exam paper as long as your final answer is clear. If writing down a word equation you have memorised helps you to answer a question then do it!

---

**6.** This question covers the concept of how the physical properties of oil fractions change. It is quite likely you will have to tackle a question on the fractional distillation or separation of crude oil – it is a topic used time and again in the General Chemistry exam.

A  1 mark

**HINT:** Crude oil is a mixture of hydrocarbons. As the boiling point of these hydrocarbons increases, their physical properties change: viscosity increases, ease of evaporation decreases and flammability decreases. Statement A is correct as the fraction containing hydrocarbons with the lowest boiling point will be the most flammable.

---

**7.** In this question you have to apply your knowledge of rusting to how you would protect iron. Questions on preventing rusting are very common in the exam. In this question an iron key is used but any iron object could be included.

A  1 mark
C  1 mark

**HINT:** When iron rusts it loses electrons. Iron can be protected by providing it with electrons to replace those it has lost. This can be done in two ways:

Box A  By attaching iron to a metal higher in the electrochemical series. The electrons will flow from the metal higher to iron. In this case electrons will flow from magnesium to iron.

Box C  By attaching iron to the negative electrode of a battery. The electrons will flow from the electrode to iron.

In box B the iron is attached to the positive electrode of a battery. This would take electrons away from iron, so it rusts. In box D the iron is attached to a metal below iron in the electrochemical series. The electrons would flow from the iron to tin and iron would rust.

**TOP EXAM TIP:** Remember the electrochemical series is on page 7 of the data booklet.

---

**8.** This is another very commonly asked type of question. It tests your knowledge of what happens in different types of chemical reactions or processes.

(a) C  1 mark

**HINT:** In a displacement reaction, a metal higher in the electrochemical series takes the place of a metal lower down. In this example, iron displaces copper.

Page 112

## Worked Answers to Practice Exam A: General Chemistry

(b) A  **1 mark**

> **HINT**: In a chemical reaction at least one new substance is made. Filtration is a technique used to separate a mixture, so no new substance is made.

(c) D  **1 mark**

> **HINT**: Fermentation of glucose is the only chemical reaction you need to learn that involves an enzyme in yeast.

### Part 2 – Written Questions

**TOP EXAM TIP**

Always look at the space for the marks to see what type of question it is. If it is Knowledge and Understanding it is asking for a piece of knowledge that you have learned. If it is Problem Solving it is either a question that you can work the answer out for or you may have to apply some of your knowledge.

★ **9.** This question is about fossil fuels. All parts are Knowledge and Understanding.

(a) Will run out **or** limited **or** non-renewable **or** not last forever  **1 mark**

(b) You must mention the following things for the 2 marks:

You get a **½ mark** for saying that coal is made from plants. Any mention of animals or sea creatures will be marked as incorrect. Another **½ mark** is for suggesting that it happened millions of years ago. It is not acceptable to say that it happened a long time ago.

For the **second mark** you must have two of the following:
- a mention of the creatures being buried
- a mention that the creatures rot or decay or turn into oil
- a mention of pressure and heat being needed (saying squashed or crushed and heated would be ok).

(c) Sulphur dioxide or nitrogen dioxide  **1 mark**

## Worked Answers to Practice Exam A: General Chemistry

> **10.** This question is based on the extraction of iron from iron ore. There is a bar chart question in the general exam every year so make sure you can draw them! Also included in this question are the commonly asked concepts of name endings in compounds, alloys and reactivity of metals.

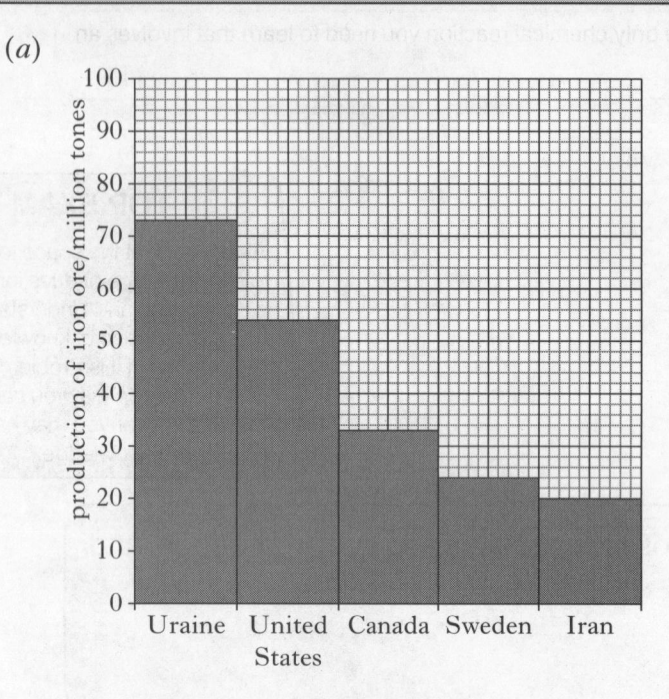

(a)

[Bar chart: production of iron ore/million tonnes on y-axis (0–100), countries on x-axis: Uraine ~73, United States ~54, Canada ~33, Sweden ~24, Iran ~20]

**TOP EXAM TIP**

When drawing a bar graph for your answer it is important to make sure each bar is exactly the correct height. Also use a pencil in case you make a mistake and a ruler for accuracy. If you feel you must start drawing the bar chart again you can use the additional graph paper at the back of the exam.

**TOP EXAM TIP**

As you can see, it is very important to make sure your graph is as clearly and accurately drawn as possible: use as much space as you can to draw the graph, label the axes, create a vertical scale on the y axis and, of course, get the bars at the right height.

The bar graph is marked in this way:

| | |
|---|---|
| The bars are drawn at the correct height: | **1 mark** |
| Production of iron ore/million tonnes and bars labelled: | **½ mark** |
| A vertical scale on the y-axis: | **½ mark** |

**HINT**

In bar graphs, marks can be taken off for a number of reasons:

- If a bar is missing or is at the incorrect height, ½ a mark will be deducted. You will only be penalised by up to 1 mark this way.
- If your graph is too small (uses less than half of the paper in either direction), ½ a mark will be deducted.
- If you draw a line graph, you will only be able to score 1 out of 2.

(b) (i) calcium, carbon and oxygen. **1 mark**

All three elements are required.

**HINT**

The ending 'ate' in calcium carbon**ate** means that it contains two elements and oxygen. There are three name endings you need to learn. In general:

- if a compound name ends in –**ide**, then it contains two elements.
- if a compound name end in –**ate** or –**ite** then it contains two elements **and** oxygen.

(ii) A mixture of metals **or** a mixture of metals and non-metals. **1 mark**

(c) An indication of more bubbles being produced. **1 mark**

**HINT**

The question suggests that you look at the Electrochemical Series in the Data Booklet. This is very similar to the Reactivity Series for metals. Because zinc is more reactive than iron, it will react more quickly, so produce more bubbles of gas.

## Worked Answers to Practice Exam A: General Chemistry

> **11.** Part (a) is a problem-solving question about an experiment involving a catalyst.
>
> In part (i) you have to look at a table of results to answer the question. In part (ii) you need to use the concept of a fair test.
>
> Part (b) is about cracking a hydrocarbon. Questions about both catalysts and cracking are very common in the General exam.

(a) (i) Manganese dioxide      **1 mark**

> **HINT** — The best catalyst will give the fastest reaction. In this case the speed of reaction is indicated by the volume of gas produced after 30 s. The greater the volume, the faster the reaction.

(ii) Temperature **or** volume of hydrogen peroxide **or** mass of catalyst.
     **1 mark**

(b) (i) Cracking      **1 mark**

(ii) $C_5H_{12}$      **1 mark**

> **HINT** — In cracking, a larger molecule is broken down into smaller molecules. X is the difference between $C_7H_{16}$ and $C_2H_4$ so $C_7-C_2 = C_5$, $H_{16}-H_4 = H_{12}$.

> **12.** This question, based on plastics, includes a flowchart. You have to read the passage about how polystyrene is made and use it to fill in the blanks in part (a). This type of problem-solving question is very common. Part (c) is also a problem-solving question and involves the construction of a table using information from a pie chart. Again, this type of problem-solving question is very common. There are also a couple of ku times about plastics in this question.

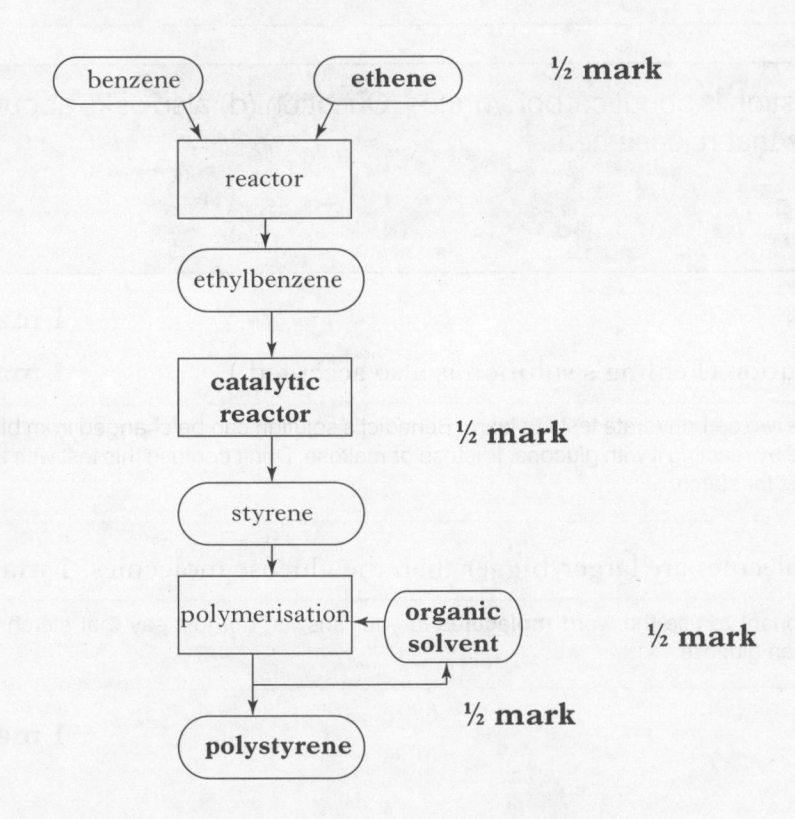

(a)

benzene + ethene    ½ **mark**
↓
reactor
↓
ethylbenzene
↓
**catalytic reactor**    ½ **mark**
↓
styrene
↓
polymerisation ← organic solvent    ½ **mark**
↓
**polystyrene**    ½ **mark**

Page 115

# Worked Answers to Practice Exam A: General Chemistry

**HINT** — Look at the two different shapes of box in the chart.

⬭ contains the name of chemicals

▭ contains the name of a reactor or process

This should help you to fill in the chart.

**TOP EXAM TIP**

If, given a paragraph of text and asked to complete a flow chart, **on the paragraph** underline the names of any chemicals and reactors/processes shown on the flow chart. This can then help you to pick out the chemicals and reactors/processes left in the paragraph that will be used to complete the flow chart.

(b) thermoplastic — **1 mark**

**HINT** — There are two types of plastic you need to learn. A **thermoplastic** softens on heating and can be reshaped. A **thermosetting** plastic cannot be reshaped on heating.

(c)

| Uses of polystyrene | % |
|---|---|
| packaging | 75 |
| drinking cups | 12 |
| insulation | 10 |
| other uses | 3 |

This table is marked in the following way:

A table is drawn: ½ mark

There are suitable/appropriate headings: ½ mark

The word percentage could be used instead of %.

The information is entered correctly into the table: 1 mark

It does not matter what order the information is entered in.

(d) Fumes are toxic **or** fumes are poisonous — **1 mark**

**HINT** — Other acceptable answers would include: fumes contain carbon monoxide/fumes can kill people. Try not to give vague answers like 'bad chemicals', 'causes pollution' or 'damages the environment'. The learning outcome this question is based on states that burning plastics creates **toxic** fumes.

★ **13.** This question is about carbohydrates. Question (d) also asks about reactions that release heat.

(a) Carbohydrates — **1 mark**

(b) Benedict's solution (Fehling's solution is also accepted.) — **1 mark**

**HINT** — There are two carbohydrate tests to learn. Benedict's solution can be changed from blue to orange by reacting it with glucose, fructose or maltose. Don't confuse this test with the iodine test for starch.

(c) The starch molecules are larger/bigger than the glucose molecules. **1 mark**

**HINT** — It is important to use the word **molecules** in your answer, not just say that starch is bigger than glucose.

(d) Exothermic — **1 mark**

# Worked Answers to Practice Exam A: General Chemistry

> **14.** This question tests your knowledge of the products of neutralisation, writing formula and precipitation reactions. There is usually one question in the exam that tests your formulae writing skills.

(a) (i) Water      **1 mark**

> **HINT** The formula, $H_2O$ would also be an acceptable answer. However if you get the formula for water incorrect you will be awarded no mark.

> **HINT** When a metal oxide reacts with an acid the products are always a salt and water. The general equation is: metal oxide + acid → a salt + water.

(ii) $K_2O$      **1 mark**

> **HINT** The chemical formula of a compound can be obtained by swapping over the valencies of the two elements.
>
> | | Potassium oxide | |
> |---|---|---|
> | Symbol | K | O |
> | Valency | 1 | 2 |
> | Swap | 2 | 1 |
> | Check for common factor | 2 | 1 |
> | Formula | $K_2O$ | |
>
> $(K^+)_2 O^{2-}$ is also acceptable.
>
> | Group number | 1 | 2 | 3 | 4 | 5 | 6 | 7 | 0 |
> |---|---|---|---|---|---|---|---|---|
> | Valency | 1 | 2 | 3 | 4 | 3 | 2 | 1 | 0 |

**TOP EXAM TIP**

Using the Periodic Table in your data book will help you find the valencies of the different elements. Remember that valency is a measure of the number of chemical bonds formed by the atoms of a given element.

(b) Barium sulphate      **1 mark**

> **HINT** This is the **precipitation** reaction that happens:
> **potassium sulphate + barium chloride → potassium chloride + barium sulphate.**
> Note that the metals have swapped place. You can now look at the solubility table on page 5 of the data booklet to find out which product is **insoluble**.

(c) It contains potassium.      **1 mark**

An answer indicating that potassium oxide is very soluble would also be acceptable.

> **HINT** Plants require three essential elements – nitrogen, potassium and phosphorous, so fertilisers contain these elements. Fertilisers also have to be soluble so plants can absorb them through their roots.

## Worked Answers to Practice Exam A: General Chemistry

**15.** There is almost always a question based on batteries. In this question you have to apply your knowledge of the electrochemical series.

(a) (i) Zinc to copper. **1 mark**

**HINT** Electrons will flow from the metal higher in the electrochemical series to the metal lower in the series.

(ii) A **1 mark**

**HINT** The further apart the metals are in the electrochemical series then the greater the voltage produced.

**TOP EXAM TIP** The electrochemical series is found on page 7 of the data book.

(b) To complete the circuit **or** to act as an electrolyte **1 mark**

**HINT** In batteries and cells ionic solutions or pastes are used as electrolytes. The electrolytes complete the circuit. Electrolytes must be ionic compounds in which the ions are free to move, i.e. solution, molten or in the form of a paste.

**16.** This question is based on acids and pH. Knowledge of the pH scale is very important.

(a) Any number between 4 and 7 **1 mark**

The number 7 is acceptable.

**HINT** When diluting an acid, its pH moves up towards 7.

(b) hydrogen or $H^+$ **1 mark**

(c) $C_6H_8O_7$ **1 mark**

Note the position of the numbers after the letters. The answer $C^6H^8O^7$ would be unacceptable. Numbers placed low after an atom, show how many of that atom there are (e.g. $H_2O$ shows that there are 2 hydrogen atoms in a water molecule).

**17.** This question is based on the chemistry of the gas ammonia, which is used to make fertilisers. Part (b) is a problem-solving question asking you to describe the trend shown by a line graph.

(a) (i) Iron **1 mark**

**HINT** The other industrial process you need to know the catalyst for is the Ostwald process. The catalyst for the Ostwald process is platinum. Try to not get the Haber process and the Ostwald process mixed up.

## Worked Answers to Practice Exam A: General Chemistry

   (ii) It increases. **1 mark**

> **HINT**: This question is asking you to say what happens to the percentage yield when the pressure increases. As the line is going up to the right, the % yield is increasing.

**TOP EXAM TIP**

When asked to describe a trend from a graph or a table, don't mention any numbers shown on the graph or in the table. Just describe the trend. Ask yourself this question: as one set of data increases, is the other increasing or decreasing?

 (b) More food required **or** more food required by populations that are large in size  **1 mark**

> **HINT**: You must mention that more food is needed in your answer. It is not enough to just mention an increased population.

 (c) Turns blue  **1 mark**

> **HINT**: Ammonia is the only **alkaline** gas you need to learn about.

★ **18.** This question is based on the electrolysis of a coloured compound. You need to apply your knowledge of ions to what is observed at the electrodes.

 (a) Carbon **or** graphite **or** C  **1 mark**

> **HINT**: Carbon in the form of graphite is the only non-metal that conducts electricity. If the electrodes do not conduct electricity then the circuit is not complete.

 (b) The breaking up of a compound using electricity  **1 mark**

> **HINT**: You must use the word '**compound**'. It is unacceptable to say that electrolysis is used to break up 'atoms', 'molecules' or 'elements'.

 (c) They are colourless.  **1 mark**

   It is **not** acceptable to use the word clear.

> **HINT**: Non-metals form negative ions. The chloride ion is negatively charged so will be attracted to the positive electrode during electrolysis.

Page 119

# PRACTICE EXAM B — WORKED ANSWERS

## Part 1 – Grid Questions

**1.** This question covers commonly asked questions about elements from the Periodic Table. Notice that parts (a), (b) and (d) guide you to the data booklet.

**TOP EXAM TIP**
The data booklet contains lots of information, including the Periodic Table. Become familiar with its contents and use it where possible to help you.

(a) C — 1 mark
(b) A — 1 mark

**HINT:** Elements that have been made by scientists are the most recently discovered. They are the elements with the largest atomic numbers and are found at the bottom of the Periodic Table. On page 8 of the data booklet they have the symbol * next to their name.

(c) D — 1 mark
(d) D and E. — 1 mark

**HINT:** The transition metals are found in the central block of the Periodic Table between groups 2 and 3. This group is labelled on page 8 of your data booklet.

**2.** This question shows you a grid containing some elements and compounds. To answer it successfully you need to recognise the type of substance from its name.

(a) A and D. — 1 mark

**HINT:** Elements are found on the Periodic Table. No other types of substances are. Use page 8 of your data booklet to look for each of the substances in the question. If they are on the Periodic Table they must be elements.

(b) F — 1 mark

**HINT:** Lime is a substance used to neutralise acidic soil and lakes.

(c) E — 1 mark

**HINT:** Methane belongs to the family of hydrocarbons called the alkanes. You need to be able to recognise the names of the first eight alkanes.

**TOP EXAM TIP**
The names of the first eight alkanes are given in the data booklet, page 6.

# Worked Answers to Practice Exam B: General Chemistry

**3.** This question tests your knowledge of different solutions used for chemical tests from across the chemistry course. There is often a question about chemical tests in the written or the grid section.

**HINT:** The solutions you need to know that are used in tests are:
1. Lime water – test for carbon dioxide
2. Bromine solution – test for unsaturation
3. Universal indicator – test for pH
4. Ferroxyl indicator – test for presence of $Fe^{2+}$ ions (indicates rusting starting)
5. Iodine solution – test for starch
6. Benedict's solution – test for glucose.

(a) A                                                                                           **1 mark**

**HINT:** Bromine solution is decolourised immediately by unsaturated hydrocarbons. An unsaturated hydrocarbon contains a carbon-to-carbon double bond. The alkenes are examples of unsaturated hydrocarbons.

(b) E                                                                                           **1 mark**

**HINT:** Benedict's solution turns from blue to an orange precipitate in the presence of glucose.

(c) F                                                                                           **1 mark**

**HINT:** Limewater turns from colourless to cloudy/milky if carbon dioxide is bubbled through it.

**TOP EXAM TIP**
Make sure you learn chemical tests.

**4.** This question tests your knowledge of various gases. Parts (a) and (c) are knowledge questions. Part (a) is based on fertilisers and part (c) on bonding. Part (b) is a problem-solving question for which you can use the data booklet to find the information.

(a) D                                                                                           **1 mark**

**HINT:** The Haber process makes ammonia ($NH_3$). The word equation is nitrogen + hydrogen → ammonia

**TOP EXAM TIP**
Don't get ammonia and ammonium mixed up - ammonia ($NH_3$) is a gas, ammonium ($NH_4^+$) is an ion.

(b) C                                                                                           **1 mark**

**HINT:** You need to look at the electron arrangements of the gases. In the data booklet on page 1 these are printed underneath the symbol for an element. The last number in an electron arrangement is the number of outer electrons. For oxygen the electron arrangement is 2,6 so oxygen has 6 outer electrons.

**TOP EXAM TIP**
On page one of the data book is a key showing what the information in each box on the Periodic Table represents.

## Worked Answers to Practice Exam B: General Chemistry

(c) A and B. **1 mark**

**HINT:** The noble gases (found in Group 0) exist as single atoms **not** joined to each other. They can be described as monatomic elements. All the other elements in the grid exist as diatomic molecules, which means their molecules contain **two** atoms.

**TOP EXAM TIP**
There are 7 diatomic elements. You must know them for your exam. They are:
- Hydrogen
- Nitrogen
- Oxygen
- Fluorine
- Chlorine
- Bromine
- Iodine

★ **5.** This problem solving question covers the concept of a fair test, which is a commonly questioned area in the exam. You need to look carefully at how each variable has changed in each experiment.

A and F **1 mark**

**HINT:** The question asks for 2 experiments to show the effect of concentration of acid on the speed of reaction. You must pick 2 experiments that have different concentrations of acid. To make sure it is a fair test **both other variables must be kept the same**. Therefore in this question, A and F are the correct answers as they have different concentrations (0.5 mol/l and 2 mol/l) but have the same temperature (20°C) and same particle size (lumps).

★ **6.** In this question, part (a) is about reactions of acids and part (b) is about a precipitation reaction. In part (b) you need to use the solubility table in the data booklet to work out the product of the precipitation reaction. This is a common problem solving question.

(a) A **1 mark**

**HINT:** Metal carbonates react with dilute acid to produce carbon dioxide gas.

(b) A and B. **1 mark**

**HINT:** When ionic solutions are mixed we can swap the positive ion (the first part of the name) around, e.g.

**ammonium carbonate + copper sulphate → copper carbonate + ammonium sulphate**

A precipitate is an insoluble solid. If either of the products in the equation is insoluble then it will be the precipitate. This information can be found on page 5 of the data booklet. In this case copper carbonate is insoluble.

**TOP EXAM TIP**
The solubility table on page 5 of the data booklet gives information on how soluble different compounds are. Make sure you know how to use it.

## Worked Answers to Practice Exam B: General Chemistry

**7.** This question shows six experiments from across the chemistry course. You need to look carefully at each diagram and identify the type of experiment.

(a) F  *1 mark*

**HINT** — Burning hydrocarbons such as methane produces carbon dioxide and water. In box B, carbon is being burned, but it would produce carbon dioxide only. Substances which contain the elements carbon and hydrogen will burn to produce carbon dioxide and water (hydrogen oxide). At general level you need to learn that hydrocarbons and carbohydrates burn to produce carbon dioxide and water.

(b) E  *1 mark*

**HINT** — When an acid reacts with an alkali, neutralisation occurs. Any reaction involving an acid is neutralisation.

(c) A  *1 mark*

**HINT** — Learn that amylase is the enzyme used to breakdown starch to glucose.

**8.** In this question, a diagram is shown of the electrolysis of an acid. You are given some statements and asked to choose the correct one. There is usually one question in the grid section which asks you to choose the correct statement or statements.

D.  *1 mark*

**HINT** — Looking at the statements in turn:

A is incorrect, as all acids **do** conduct electricity as they contain many ions.

B is incorrect, as the pH of acids are **below** 7.

C is incorrect, as acids are ionic so contain many ions.

D is correct as all acids contain hydrogen ions ($H^+$). Because the hydrogen ions in acids are positively charged, they are attracted to the negative electrode. When **any** acid undergoes electrolysis, hydrogen gas is produced at the negative electrode.

**TOP EXAM TIP**

In questions where you are asked to choose from statements, look at each statement in turn. Mark down next to the statement whether you think a statement is correct with a tick or wrong with a cross. If you are unsure about a statement put a question mark opposite it. This can help you to eliminate wrong answers quickly and focus on finding the correct answer (or answers).

## Part 2 – Written Questions

**9.** This question is about plastics. All three parts cover commonly asked concepts. To answer part (d) you need to understand what a property is.

(a) Propene.  *1 mark*

## Worked Answers to Practice Exam B: General Chemistry

**HINT** — In a polymer, the name of the monomer is in the brackets with the word poly in front of it.

(b) Melts on heating **or** softens on heating **or** can be reshaped on heating

**1 mark**

(c) Electrical insulator **or** does not conduct electricity **or** flexible.

**HINT** — PVC must not conduct electricity, otherwise someone who touched the covered wire would get a shock.

**TOP EXAM TIP**
You should be able to link everyday uses of plastics to their properties.

10. This question is based on the gas argon. There are a couple of knowledge questions on families of the Periodic Table and structure of the atom. Part (c) is a problem-solving question which uses the skill of describing a trend from a table. Describing a trend from a table or graph is commonly asked in the exam.

(a) Noble gases

**1 mark**

**HINT** — You must ensure that you know the names and positions of the following groups on the Periodic Table.

| Group Number | Group Name |
|---|---|
| 1 | Alkali metals |
| 7 | Halogens |
| 8 or 0 | Noble gases |
| Between 2 and 3 | Transition metals |

(b)

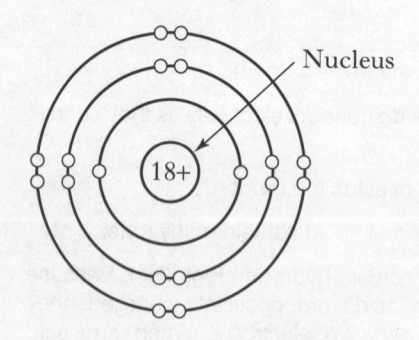

[Diagram of argon atom: nucleus labelled 18+, with three electron shells containing 2, 8, and 8 electrons]

**1 mark**

**HINT** — The nucleus is the positively charged centre of an atom. The electrons move around the nucleus.

(c) Density increases **or** density gets bigger.

**1 mark**

**HINT** — When answering a question that asks about a trend or pattern, look for a general pattern. Do not describe each number in detail.

## Worked Answers to Practice Exam B: General Chemistry

> **11.** This question is about the fermentation of glucose to make alcohol. Part (b) is testing the problem-solving skill of presenting information from a passage as a table. This is a very commonly tested skill. In part (d) you are asked to write a formula.

(a) Ethanol **1 mark**

(b) (i)

| Drink | Plant source |
|---|---|
| Gin | Juniper Berries |
| Vodka | Potatoes |
| Whisky | Barley |
| Wine | Grapes |

A table is marked in the following way:

A table is drawn: ½ mark
There are suitable headings: ½ mark
The information is entered correctly into the table: **1 mark**
(½ a mark can be deducted for each incorrect or missing pair of entries up to a maximum of 1 mark.)

> **HINT:** When constructing a table, decide on the headings first. The first sentence 'Alcoholic drinks can be made from many plants' gives the two headings to be used. Then go through the passage and cross out the information in the passage as you put it in the table. This can help you not to miss out any information.

(ii) Distillation **1 mark**

> **HINT:** Water and alcohol have different boiling points so can be separated by distillation. This will increase the alcohol concentration. A useful memory aid may be that whiskey is made in a **distillery** so distillation is the process required.

(c) $SO_2$ **1 mark**

> **HINT:** When a compound's name has a number prefix (like mono-, di-, tri- or tetra-) use this to work out the formula. In this case sulphur **di**oxide means "a sulphur and **2** oxygens" thus, $SO_2$.

**TOP EXAM TIP**
In a formula the numbers must be a subscript e.g. $SO_2$ not SO2.

**TOP EXAM TIP**
The prefixes to write formula are:

| Prefix | Meaning |
|---|---|
| mono- | 1 |
| di- | 2 |
| tri- | 3 |
| tetra- | 4 |

> **12.** This question has a couple of commonly asked questions on batteries. Part (c) has a pie chart to be labelled.

(a) Any answer that suggests that batteries are safer **or** portable **or** lightweight and small. **1 mark**

## Worked Answers to Practice Exam B: General Chemistry

> **HINT** — Batteries are not cheaper than electricity. Using mains electricity is a much cheaper source of energy than batteries. Not all batteries are rechargeable and mains electricity is a continuous source of electricity.

(b) The chemicals run out **or** the chemicals are used up.  **1 mark**

(c)

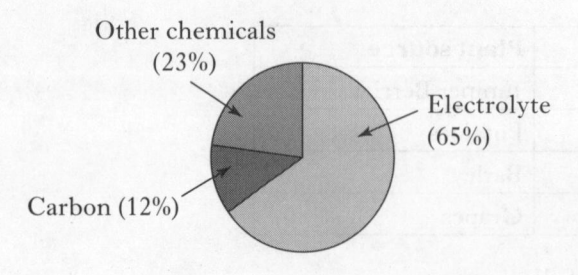

Other chemicals (23%)
Electrolyte (65%)
Carbon (12%)

Other chemicals,  ½ **mark**
23%  ½ **mark**
carbon, 12%  ½ **mark**
electrolyte, 65%  ½ **mark**

> **HINT** — The parts of a pie chart must add up to 100%.
> 65% + 12% = 77%,
> 100% − 77% = 23%
> Therefore 23% is other chemicals.

**TOP EXAM TIP**
Make sure you understand how to work out the percentage parts of a pie chart.

★ **13.** This question is based around fertilisers and essential nutrients for growth. However part (a) asks for the meaning of 'synthetic' which you may have first come across when learning about plastics.

(a) (i) Any answer that suggests made by humans **or** by the chemical industry or made in factories **or** is not natural.  **1 mark**

> **HINT** — Man-made would be an acceptable answer also. You cannot say made from chemicals as both natural and synthetic materials are made from chemicals. Do **not** say made from oil as only plastics and synthetic fibres are made from oil.

(ii) Insoluble **or** does not dissolve.  **1 mark**

> **HINT** — Plants take the nutrients in through their roots. Fertilisers must be soluble. Page 5 of the data booklet has the information that zinc phosphate is insoluble.

(b) Roots **or** root nodules  **1 mark**

> **HINT** — Plants that have these root nodules include peas, beans and clover.

## Worked Answers to Practice Exam B: General Chemistry

**14.** This question is about the conductivity of ionic compounds. Conductivity of substances is a commonly examined concept at General level. Often there will be a diagram showing an electrolysis experiment.

(a) Electrolysis **1 mark**

> **HINT** Electrolysis is the splitting up of a compound by passing electricity through it. The question mentions the phrase 'split up' and the diagram shows electricity being passed through the compound lead bromide.

(b) Lead **1 mark**

> **HINT** In a metal compound the metal ions are always positively charged. They are attracted to a negative electrode.

(c) Ions are free to move. **1 mark**

It is not acceptable to say that particles, electrons or charged particles are able to move. You must say ions.

(d) Conducts electricity **1 mark**

Other acceptable answers are insoluble **or** unreactive.

**15.** This question is based on speed of reactions. There are often questions about gas tests and catalysts in the exam. To answer part (c) correctly you need to be able to use line graphs.

(a) 3 **1 mark**

> **HINT** Catalysts speed up a reaction and are not used up in a reaction. There will always be the same mass of a catalyst at the end as there was at the start of a reaction. The diagram shows 3 g of catalyst.

(b) Relights a glowing splint **1 mark**

> **HINT** There is usually at least one gas test question in an exam.

(c) (i) 20 **1 mark**

> **HINT** Be as accurate as you can when reading from the graph.

(ii) Steeper line at start **½ mark**
Finish at the same level **½ mark**

Page 127

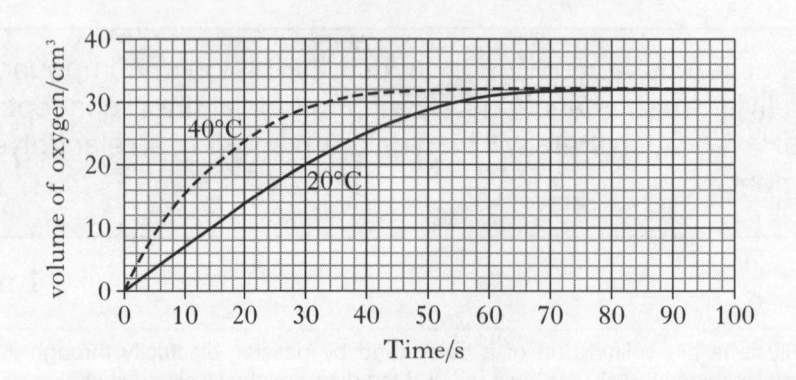

## Worked Answers to Practice Exam B: General Chemistry

> **HINT**
> The temperature of 40°C is higher than the original temperature of 20°C. Therefore the reaction will be faster. To show a reaction going faster a steeper slope is drawn.
>
> Because there is the same quantity of chemicals at the start, the same volume of oxygen gas will be produced. To show this, the line should finish at the same level.

**16.** This question is asking about the concept of reactivity of metals and uses the example of metals reacting with acid. Reactivity of metals is commonly examined at General level.

(a) B, A, C **1 mark**

> **HINT**
> The more bubbles there are, the faster the reaction. The faster the reaction, the more reactive the metal.

(b) Copper **or** mercury **or** silver **or** gold **or** platinum **1 mark**

> **HINT**
> No bubbles means that no reaction is happening. copper and the metals below it in the reactivity series do not react with dilute acid.

**TOP EXAM TIP**
The order of the reactivity series is similar to the electrochemical series on page 7 of the data booklet.

(c) Hydrogen **1 mark**

> **HINT**
> When metals react with acid they give off hydrogen gas. The general word equation is:
> metal + acid → a salt + hydrogen

**17.** This question is based on rusting experiments.

(a) (i) More blue in test tube B (salt water)
*or* less blue in test tube A (tap water) **1 mark**

> **HINT**
> Ferroxyl indicator turns from yellow to blue when rusting occurs. The more blue colour there is the more rusting has occurred. Salt water increases the speed of rusting, so there will be more blue in test tube B.

(a) (ii) $Fe^{2+}$ **or** iron(II) **1 mark**

## Worked Answers to Practice Exam B: General Chemistry

> **HINT** — When iron starts to rust, each iron atom loses two electrons (Fe changes into $Fe^{2+}$). The $Fe^{2+}$ ions turn ferroxyl indicator from yellow to blue.

(b) Any one from:  magnesium
 aluminium
 zinc                                                      **1 mark**

> **HINT** — A metal above iron in the Electrochemical Series can protect it from rusting by giving it electrons. The metal used cannot be above magnesium as it would be too reactive with water.

⭐ **18.** This question is based around the hydrocarbon butane. It includes the commonly-examined problem-solving skill of drawing a bar chart. In part (c) you need to be able to draw the full structural formula of a hydrocarbon.

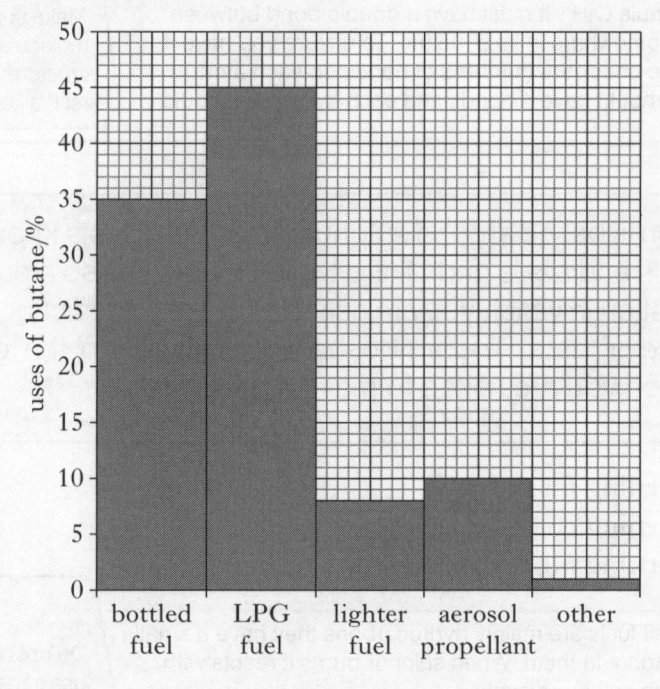

[Bar graph: y-axis "uses of butane/%" from 0 to 50; x-axis categories: bottled fuel (35), LPG fuel (45), lighter fuel (8), aerosol propellant (10), other (1)]

The bar graph is marked in this way:

Uses of butane labelled on *x*-axis and all bars labelled: **½ mark**

You have a vertical scale on the *y*-axis: **½ mark**

The bars are drawn at the correct height: **1 mark**

**TOP EXAM TIP** — When drawing a bar graph for your answer it is important to make sure each bar is exactly the correct height. Another common mistake is forgetting to label the axes.

> **HINT** — In bar graphs, marks can be taken off for a number of reasons:
> - If a bar is missing or is at the incorrect height, ½ a mark will be deducted. You will only be penalised up to 1 mark this way.
> - If your graph is too small (uses less than half of the paper in either direction), ½ a mark will be deducted.
> - If you draw a line graph, you will only be able to score 1 out of 2.

(b) A chemical that burns to give out heat or a chemical that combusts to give out heat.                                                                    **1 mark**

(c) (i) Addition                                                                  **1 mark**

Page 129

## Worked Answers to Practice Exam B: General Chemistry

**HINT:** Butene is an alkene. Alkenes can react with hydrogen (H$_2$) in an addition reaction. In this reaction, the hydrogen adds across the carbon to carbon double bond to make one molecule, an alkane and nothing else. In the example of butene and hydrogen the formula equation is;

$$C_4H_8 + H_2 \rightarrow C_4H_{10}$$

**TOP EXAM TIP:** There are many different types of chemical reaction in the Chemistry course. Make sure you learn their names.

(ii) Any of these structures. **1 mark**

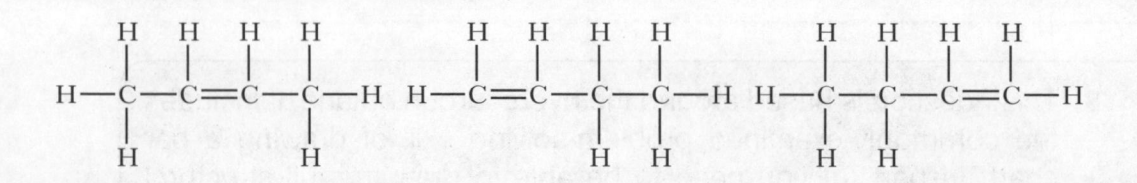

```
    H H H H        H H H H        H H H H
    | | | |        | | | |        | | | |
H—C—C=C—C—H   H—C=C—C—C—H    H—C—C—C=C—H
    |   |          |   | |      | |   
    H   H          H   H H      H H   
```

**HINT:** Remember that the ending 'ene' tells you that the chemical is an alkene. Butene has four carbons atoms in it and has the molecular formula C$_4$H$_8$. It must have a double bond between two carbons somewhere in its structure. To ensure you have it correct, double-check the numbers of bonds on each atom. Each carbon should have 4 bonds and each hydrogen should have 1 bond.

**TOP EXAM TIP:** Make sure you know the names, molecular formula and can draw structures for the first 8 alkanes and the first 6 alkenes.

**19.** This question is based around sulphur dioxide and tests knowledge from the fuels and acids and alkalis topics. There is also a problem-solving question in which you are asked to make a prediction based upon a table of data. There is usually a question in the general exam in which you are asked to make a prediction.

(a) One from:    Burning fossil fuels    **1 mark**
                 Burning coal
                 Burning oil/petrol/diesel

**HINT:** Although fossil fuels are mainly hydrocarbons they have a small amount of sulphur in them. When sulphur burns it reacts with oxygen to form sulphur dioxide.

**TOP EXAM TIP:** Do not confuse the word 'source' with 'use'. The source of something is where it comes from.

(b) (i) A number between 30 and 50    **1 mark**

**HINT:** The solubility is decreasing as the temperature increases. When you are asked to predict a value try to follow the pattern suggested by the rest of the values.

(ii) acidic    **1 mark**

**HINT:** Acidic solutions turn universal indicator red/orange/yellow.

*Page 130*

# PRACTICE EXAM C — WORKED ANSWERS

## Part 1 – Grid Questions

**1.** This question covers commonly asked questions on elements. Notice that parts (a) and (c) guide you to the Periodic Table in the data booklet. Part (b) is a question on galvanising and part (d) is about covalent bonding.

(a) A — 1 mark

**HINT:** The key on page 8 of the data booklet tells us that the top number in each box is the atomic number. The answer, lithium has an atomic number of 3. To help you identify the correct answer, you could write each atomic number beside the element in the grid.

(b) E — 1 mark

**HINT:** Galvanising with zinc is a method of preventing iron from corroding.

(c) D — 1 mark

**HINT:** The key on page 2 of the data booklet will tell you which number is density. The answer, silver has a density of 10.5. To help you identify the correct answer, you could write each density beside the element in the grid.

(d) B and F — 1 mark

**HINT:** Covalent bonds are formed between **non-metal** elements. If a metal joins with a non-metal then an ionic bond is formed.

**TOP EXAM TIP**
The zigzag line on the Periodic Table separates the metals from non-metals. There are arrows beneath the zigzag line which inform you of this. The non-metals are found to the right of this line. The exception to this is hydrogen, which is a non-metal but appears in group 1.

**2.** This question is on the hydrocarbon families, the alkanes and the alkenes.

(a) A and B — 1 mark

**HINT:** Alkanes names end in '-ane'. Alkenes end in '-ene'.

(b) F — 1 mark

**TOP EXAM TIP**
Make sure you know what information is in the data booklet. Page 6 contains some information for Standard Grade candidates and some for use by Intermediate 2 candidates. Make sure you know what information is for Standard Grade candidates.

*Page 131*

## Worked Answers to Practice Exam C: General Chemistry

(c) C  **1 mark**

**HINT:** Propene has 3 carbons. However the first alkene is ethene because there must be a carbon-to-carbon double bond. Methene cannot exist. Therefore propene is the second member of the alkene family.

**TOP EXAM TIP:** You should know the names of the first eight alkanes and the first six alkenes.

⭐ **3.** Name endings in compounds and elements present in fertilisers are both popular exam topics at General level.

(a) A and D  **1 mark**

**HINT:** If a compound contains 2 elements then its name will end in '-ide'. If its name ends in '-ate' or '-ite' then it has at least 3 elements. One of these must be oxygen.

(b) E  **1 mark**

**HINT:** Plants require the essential elements nitrogen, phosphorus and potassium. All fertilisers will contain at least one of these. Normally the nitrogen is in the form of nitrates or ammonium compounds. Phosphates provide the phosphorus and potassium compounds provide the potassium.

**TOP EXAM TIP:** The formulae for ions whose names end in 'ate' or 'ite' are found on page 4 of the data booklet. The formulae for ammonium and hydroxide ions are also there.

⭐ **4.** This question uses the pH scale as the basis of a question. Knowledge of the pH scale is very important as it forms the basis of many questions about acids and alkalis.

(a) A and B  **1 mark**

**HINT:** Acids have a pH less than 7. When diluted the pH moves towards 7, i.e. the pH increases.

(b) A  **1 mark**

**HINT:** The lower the pH, the more acidic a substance is.

**TOP EXAM TIP:** Learn the pH scale.

⭐ **5.** It is important to learn the names of chemical reactions and processes. This type of grid question has appeared in the exam a few times in the last few years. Being asked to name a chemical reaction is also a popular question in the written section.

(a) E  **1 mark**

**HINT:** Chlorophyll is the green chemical found in plants which traps energy from the sun. Light energy is required during photosynthesis.

## Worked Answers to Practice Exam C: General Chemistry

(b)  A    **1 mark**

> **HINT**  Plastics are examples of **polymers** so the type of reaction used to make them is **polymer**isation.

(c)  B    **1 mark**

**6.** This question is about the different methods used to prevent the rusting of iron.

(a)  D    **1 mark**

> **HINT**  Oiling/greasing is a suitable method for protecting something that is required to move.

**7.** This question covers several aspects about the reactivity of metals. It is asking you to pick the correct statement. There is usually one question in the grid section that asks you to select the answer or answers from a list of statements.

### TOP EXAM TIP
Sometimes statement questions have one answer, sometimes two answers. If there is one answer the question will say 'Identify the correct statement'. If there is two answers the question will say 'Identify the **two** correct statements.'

D    **1 mark**

> **HINT**  Page 7 of the data booklet is very useful here. Since **the electrochemical series is very similar to the reactivity series** we can use it to show that zinc is fairly reactive and silver is unreactive. Taking the other statements in turn:
>
> A is incorrect, only the most unreactive metals are found uncombined in the Earth.
> B is incorrect, only very reactive metals react with water.
> C is incorrect, only metals above iron in the electrochemical series will be used to provide sacrificial protection.
> D is correct, both zinc and silver are below magnesium in the reactivity series.
> E is incorrect, only very reactive metals are stored under oil.

### TOP EXAM TIP
The order of metals in the reactivity series is very similar to the electrochemical series on page 7 of the data booklet.

**8.** This question tests your knowledge of various gases studied during the course. Part (a) is about poisonous gases and part (b) is about respiration.

(a)  F    **1 mark**

> **HINT**  There are three poisonous gases to learn at general level: carbon monoxide, sulphur dioxide and nitrogen dioxide.

## Worked Answers to Practice Exam C: General Chemistry

(b) D     **1 mark**

> **HINT**
> Learn the word equation for respiration and you can answer this question:
> glucose + oxygen → carbon dioxide + water
>
> You should know that this is the reverse of photosynthesis:
> carbon dioxide + water → glucose + oxygen

★ **9.** This question is about the commonly-examined concept of electrical conductivity of substances.

B     **1 mark**

C     **1 mark**

> **HINT**
> To answer this type of question you need to know the rules for substances conducting electricity.
>
> **For Elements:** All metal elements conduct electricity. All non-metals do not, except carbon in the form of graphite. Therefore gold (metal) does conduct and iodine (non-metal) does not conduct.
>
> **For Compounds:** Ionic compounds conduct when the ions are free to move i.e. when molten or in solution but **not** when solid. Covalent compounds never conduct. Therefore molten lead bromide (molten ionic) does conduct while molten sucrose (covalent) does not.

> **TOP EXAM TIP**
> You can recognise the type of bonding a compound has by the elements it is made up from. Covalent compounds contain non-metals only. Ionic compounds usually contain a metal or ammonium.

## Part 2 – Written Questions

★ **10.** This question is on the structure of the atom and families of the Periodic Table. You need to use your knowledge of electron arrangements to answer part (a).

(a)

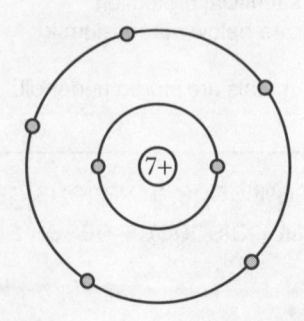

2 electrons in the first shell.

5 electrons in the second shell.     **1 mark**

> **HINT**
> The arrangement of electrons around the nucleus is given on page 1 of the data booklet. The example given in the question, lithium, has the electron arrangement 2,1. There are 2 electrons in the first shell and 1 in the second shell. It follows that nitrogen with the electron arrangement 2,5 will have 2 electrons in the first shell and 5 electrons in the second shell.

## Worked Answers to Practice Exam C: General Chemistry

(b) Alkali metals **1 mark**

> **HINT** Group 1 elements are called the alkali metals.

> ⭐ **11.** This question is based on fractional distillation. Often there will be a diagram of a fractionating tower in this sort of question.

(a) (i) Naphtha **1 mark**

> **HINT** For questions on fuels you should know the fractions in order. Try to use a mnemonic. As the boiling point of these fractions increases, flammability decreases. Hence as naphtha has a lower boiling point than kerosene it is more flammable.

> **TOP EXAM TIP**
> Information from diagrams can help you to answer questions.

(ii) Kerosene **1 mark**

> **HINT** You should also know at least 1 use for every fraction.

(b) Hydrogen **and** carbon **1 mark**

If you include **any** other elements it will be marked incorrect.

> ⭐ **12.** This question includes a flowchart. You have to read the passage about how lead is extracted and use it to fill in the blanks. This type of problem-solving question is very common. Part (b) involves the working out of a percentage. There is usually one question in the paper that involves simple maths. Part (c) uses the skill of writing a word equation and part (d) is about batteries.

(a)

impure lead sulphide → oven → **sulphides** (½ mark), silicates
oven → **lead oxide** (½ mark)
**carbon** (½ mark) → furnace → carbon dioxide
furnace → impure lead
**electrolysis** (½ mark) → impurities
electrolysis → pure lead

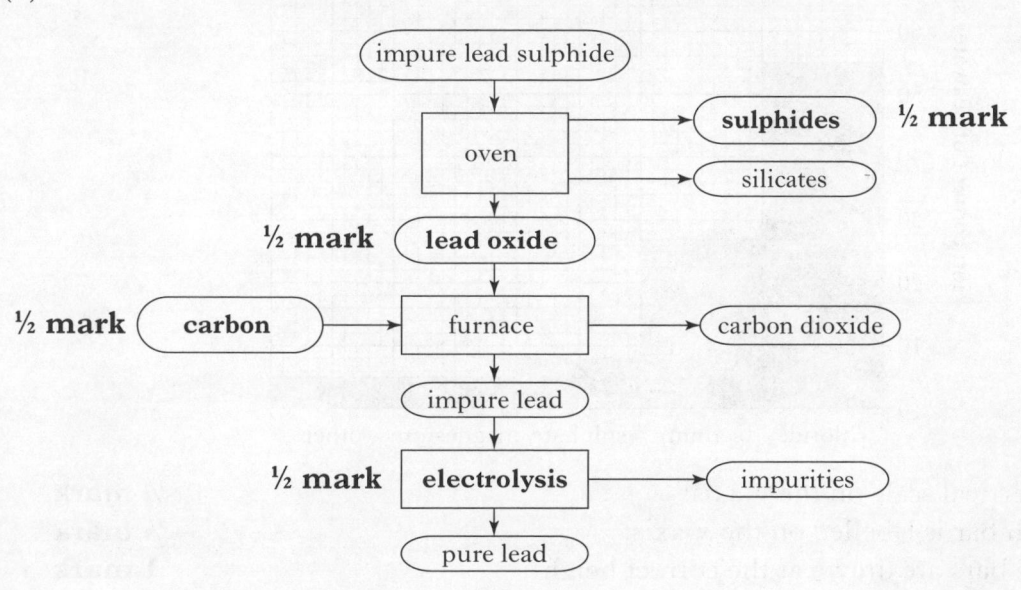

Page 135

## Worked Answers to Practice Exam C: General Chemistry

**HINT:** Look at the two different shapes of box in the chart.
⬭ contains the name of chemicals
▭ contains the name of a reactor or process

**TOP EXAM TIP**
A problem-solving question may be based on information you have not come across before. Don't panic! Just read the question carefully.

(b) 2     **1 mark**

**HINT:** To work out a percentage: 8 × 25 ÷ 100 =

**TOP EXAM TIP**
It is useful to have a calculator.

(c) lead oxide + carbon → lead + carbon dioxide     **1 mark**

**HINT:** The substances reacting appear on the left of the arrow and the substances produced appear on the right.

(d) To complete the circuit     **1 mark**

**HINT:** The purpose of an electrolyte or ion-bridge in any battery or cell is to complete the circuit.

---

**13.** In part (a) of this question a bar chart is to be drawn from the information on a pie chart. In part (b) the formula for a compound is to be worked out. Both drawing a bar chart and writing a formula are extremely popular questions.

(a)

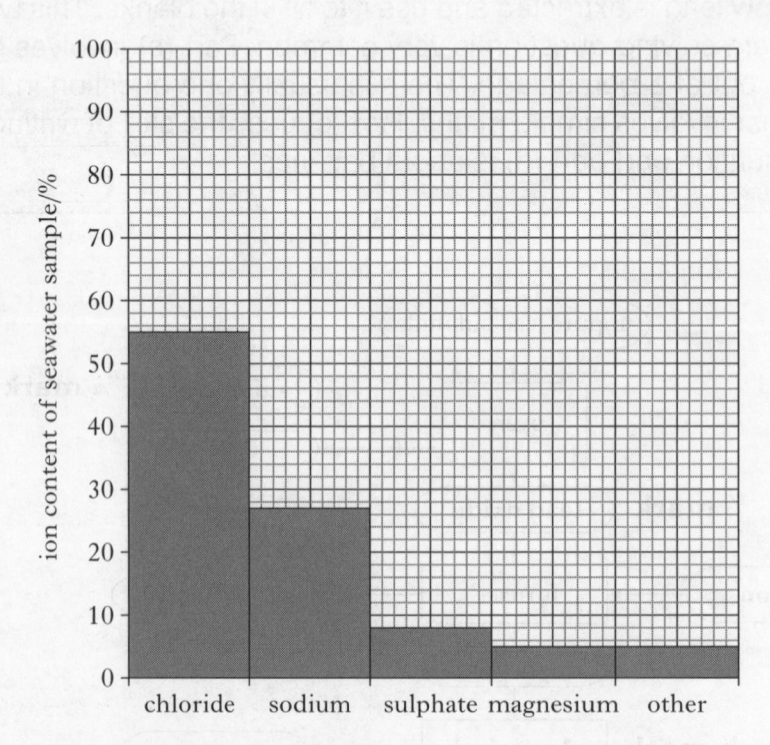

[Bar chart showing ion content of seawater sample/% on y-axis (0–100) with bars for: chloride ~55, sodium ~27, sulphate ~8, magnesium ~5, other ~5]

A vertical scale on the y-axis:     **½ mark**
Each bar is labelled on the x-axis:     **½ mark**
The bars are drawn at the correct height:     **1 mark**

(b) $MgSO_4$   **or**   $Mg^{2+}SO_4^{2-}$     **1 mark**

## Worked Answers to Practice Exam C: General Chemistry

**HINT:** The chemical formula of a compound can be obtained by swapping over the valencies of the two ions. The sulphate ion contains more than one kind of atom and so its formula is found on page 4 of the data booklet. The size of the charge on the ion gives the valency. The sulphate ion is $SO_4^{2-}$, so its valency is 2.

|  | Magnesium Sulphate |  |
|---|---|---|
| Symbol | Mg | SO$_4$ |
| Valency | 2 | 2 |
| Swap | 2 | 2 |
| Check for common factor | 1 | 1 |
| Formula | MgSO$_4$ |  |

**TOP EXAM TIP:** The formulae for ions containing more than one kind of atom can be found on page 4 of the data booklet. The charge on the ion gives the ion's valency.

**14.** This question is based around alloys. There is usually at least one mark on alloys in the general paper. In part (b) you need to relate the property of an alloy to its use. In part (c) you are asked to make a prediction, which is a commonly examined problem-solving skill.

(a) Alloy — **1 mark**

(b) Any from:
light
lightweight
low density
does not corrode
unreactive
hardwearing. — **1 mark**

**HINT:** Try to think of the most obvious property. Planes need to lift off into the sky so they need to be as light as possible

**TOP EXAM TIP:** You should be able to link everyday uses of alloys and metals to their properties.

(c) A number between 200 and 225 — **1 mark**

**15.** This question is based around compounds containing sulphur.

Part (a) tests you knowledge of the terms used to describe a solution. In part (b) the chemical reaction precipitation is the basis for the question. In part (c) you are asked to come up with a rule for solubility using information from the table and the Periodic Table.

(a) Solute — **1 mark**

**HINT:** A solution is formed when a solute dissolves in a solvent. As zinc sulphate is dissolving it must be the solute. Water is the solvent.

(b) (i) Any from: ammonium carbonate
potassium carbonate
lithium carbonate
sodium carbonate. — **1 mark**

## Worked Answers to Practice Exam C: General Chemistry

> **HINT** — Insoluble salts are made by precipitation. The salt in this question is zinc carbonate. This is made by mixing a solution containing zinc with a solution containing carbonate. Solution X must contain the carbonate ion. Look up the solubility table on page 5 of the data booklet to find a **soluble** carbonate compound.

(ii) Filtration **or** filtering                                                  **1 mark**

A description of how to filter would also be acceptable.

> **HINT** — Filtration is a technique used to separate a solid from a liquid or a solution.

(c) They are insoluble.                                                            **1 mark**

> **HINT** — Use the Periodic Table to look up the metals in the sulphides. You could put a mark beside all the transition metals in the table. This would help you to see a pattern. The metals zinc, copper and silver are all transition metals. From the table in the question we can see that all the sulphides containing these metals are insoluble.

---

**16.** This question is based around plastics.

(a) Thermosetting plastic                                                          **1 mark**

> **HINT** — There are two types of plastics – thermosetting and thermoplastic.

(b) An answer which suggests it will not rot away or decay or decompose or a suggestion it will last longer.

> **HINT** — Biodegradable means 'it can rot away' so **non**-biodegradable means 'it **cannot** rot away'

(c) Poly(vinylchloride)                                                            **1 mark**

> **HINT** — To name a polymer, put 'poly' in front of the name of the monomer. The monomer name should go in brackets.

---

**17.** This question is based around a metal carbonate reacting with acid. In part (a) you are expected to name the type of reaction, in part (b) you are asked for a gas test and in part (c) the concept of a fair test comes up. All three of these concepts come up often in the exam.

(a) Neutralisation                                                                 **1 mark**

## Worked Answers to Practice Exam C: General Chemistry

> **HINT:** You should know all of the reactions of acids. There are four general word equations that are helpful.
>
> metal + acid → salt + hydrogen
> metal oxide + acid → salt + water
> metal hydroxide + acid → salt + water
> metal carbonate + acid → salt + water + carbon dioxide

(b) Turns limewater cloudy/milky **1 mark**

> **HINT:** There is usually at least one gas test question in an exam.

(c)

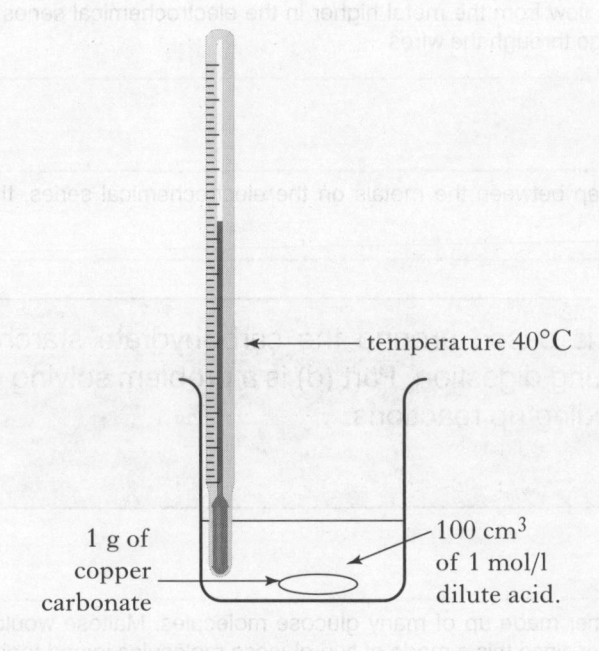

[Diagram: thermometer showing temperature 40°C in a beaker containing 1 g of copper carbonate and 100 cm³ of 1 mol/l dilute acid.]

40°C / 1 g / 100 cm³ – all three for **1 mark**

> **HINT:** In this fair test only temperature should change. The other variables **must** be kept the same.

---

**18.** This question is based on making a cell from two different metals placed in solutions of their metal ions. Parts (b) and (c) are commonly asked problem-solving questions about cells/batteries.

---

(a) Ion-bridge **1 mark**

> **HINT:** An ion-bridge is usually a piece of filter paper soaked in an electrolyte. Its job is to complete the circuit.

*Page 139*

## Worked Answers to Practice Exam C: General Chemistry

(b)

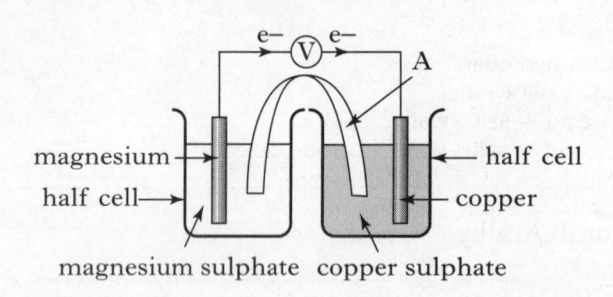

magnesium half cell ← → half cell copper

magnesium sulphate    copper sulphate

The arrow goes from Mg to Fe, through the **wires**.  **1 mark**

> **HINT** Electrons always flow from the metal higher in the electrochemical series to the metal lower. Electrons go through the wires.

(c) Silver  **1 mark**

> **HINT** The larger the gap between the metals on the electrochemical series, the larger the voltage obtained.

**19.** This question is based around the carbohydrate starch and its breakdown during digestion. Part (d) is a problem solving question based on speeding up reactions.

(a) glucose  **1 mark**

> **HINT** Starch is a polymer made up of many glucose molecules. Maltose would also be an acceptable answer since this a made of two glucose molecules joined together.

(b) (i) enzyme  **1 mark**

(ii) Blue/black colour  **1 mark**

> **HINT** The test for starch is that it turns iodine solution blue/black.

(iii) increase the rate **or** speeds up  **1 mark**

> **HINT** There are four ways to speed up a chemical reaction.
> 1. Add a catalyst
> 2. Decrease the particle size (this is the same as increasing the surface area)
> 3. Increasing the concentration
> 4. Increasing the temperature

**20.** This question is based around sparking of air. It includes a question on pH of oxides and a question on bonding.

(a) (i) Nitrogen is unreactive.  **1 mark**

## Worked Answers to Practice Exam C: General Chemistry

> **HINT** A large amount of energy is required to get nitrogen and oxygen to react. In nature this can be supplied by a lightening strike.

    (ii) Turns red/pink/orange        **1 mark**

> **HINT** All non-metal oxides are acidic when dissolved in water.

(b) Any from: two atoms joined

        made up of two atoms

        molecule made from two atoms     **1 mark**

> **21.** In this problem-solving question you have to look at how the structures and names of the compounds are changing to allow you to fill in the missing pieces of information. You also need to have knowledge of prefixes used in compound names. There are also a couple of knowledge questions on a catalyst and unsaturation.

(a) (i) It speeds up the reaction *or* it allows the reaction to happen at a lower temperature.     **1 mark**

It is unacceptable to say the catalyst can be reused *without* mentioning speeding up.

    (ii) Contains a carbon-to-carbon double bond.     **1 mark**

(b) (i)

$$\begin{array}{c} \text{Cl} \quad \text{H} \\ | \quad\quad | \\ \text{Cl}-\text{C}-\text{C}-\text{H} \\ | \quad\quad | \\ \text{H} \quad \text{Cl} \end{array} \qquad \begin{array}{c} \text{Cl} \quad \text{H} \\ | \quad\quad | \\ \text{Cl}-\text{C}-\text{C}-\text{H} \\ | \quad\quad | \\ \text{Cl} \quad \text{H} \end{array}$$

Either molecule is fine.     **1 mark**

> **HINT** Follow the pattern in the last column of the table. Following the pattern, **tri**chloromethane has **three** H atoms replaced by Cl atoms.

    (ii) Tetrachloroethane     **1 mark**

> **HINT** The prefixes and their meanings are:
>
> | Prefix | Meaning |
> |---|---|
> | mono- | 1 |
> | di- | 2 |
> | tri- | 3 |
> | tetra- | 4 |
>
> Following the pattern in the table, the molecule with **four** Cl atoms will be **tetra**chloroethane.

# PRACTICE EXAM D — WORKED ANSWERS

## Part 1 – Grid Questions

> 1. This question tests your knowledge of various elements. You need to use the data booklet for parts (a) and (c).

(a) E  **1 mark**

**HINT:** Halogens are found in group 7 of the Periodic Table.

(b) B  **1 mark**

**HINT:** Air is a mixture of several gases. Nitrogen makes up most of the air with 78%. Oxygen makes up 21% of the air. There is slightly less than 1% argon and tiny percentages of others including water and carbon dioxide.

(c) A  **1 mark**

**HINT:** Use the key on page 3 of the data booklet to help find the melting point.

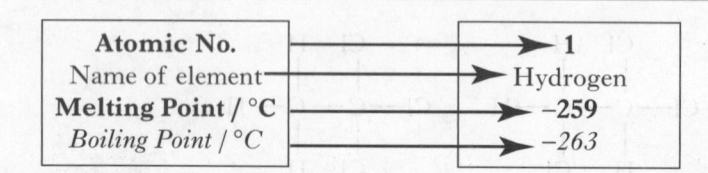

```
Atomic No. ─────────→ 1
Name of element ─────→ Hydrogen
Melting Point / °C ──→ −259
Boiling Point / °C ──→ −263
```

(d) D  **1 mark**

**HINT:** Unreactive metals are found uncombined in the Earth's crust. These are at the bottom of the reactivity series.

> 2. This question tests your knowledge of how to speed up a chemical reaction.

(a) B  **1 mark**

**HINT:** There are 4 ways to speed up a chemical reaction:
- Make the particles smaller. (increase the surface area.)
- Increase the temperature of the reaction.
- Increase the concentration.
- Use a catalyst.

In this question you can see that the particle size and the temperature change between the diagrams. In order to select the quickest reaction we must find the reaction with the smallest particles and the highest temperature.

Page 142

# Worked Answers to Practice Exam D: General Chemistry

**3.** Hydrocarbon questions in the grid part of the exam are common.

(a)  B + C     **1 mark**

**HINT** — Alkanes are the only series where to work out the number of hydrogens you double the number of carbons and add 2. This is normally written as a *general formula*, $C_nH_{2n+2}$.

(b)  A     **1 mark**

**HINT** — Propene has 3 carbons. The general formula for the alkenes is $C_nH_{2n}$. This means that propene has 6 hydrogens.

**TOP EXAM TIP**

The data booklet on page 6 has the names of the first eight alkanes and first five alkenes. You need to know the first **eight** alkanes and first **six** alkenes. Remember that you also need to be able to recognise and write their molecular and structural formula.

**4.** Sometimes part of the Periodic Table is shown in a question with letters to represent certain elements. The letters are <u>not</u> the symbols. This is mentioned in the question.

**TOP EXAM TIP**

Read each question carefully.

(a)  B + C     **1 mark**

**HINT** — Elements with similar chemical properties will be in the same group. A group on the Periodic Table is a column. A row is called a period.

(b)  A     **1 mark**

**HINT** — The alkali metals are found in group 1 of the Periodic Table. The group numbers are given in the question here and on pages 1 and 8 in the data booklet.

(c)  B     **1 mark**

**HINT** — Use page 1 of your data booklet to find out which element each letter represents. Letter B is in the position of magnesium and therefore represents the element with the electron arrangement of 2,8,2.

# Worked Answers to Practice Exam D: General Chemistry

**5.** This question tests your knowledge on various substances.

(a) F — 1 mark

**HINT:** The catalysts in car exhaust systems are made of the expensive transition metals platinum and rhodium. In this case, only platinum is mentioned so only select this.

(b) A — 1 mark

**HINT:** Crude oil is a mixture of hydrocarbons.

(c) B — 1 mark

**HINT:** Fertilisers must contain at least one of nitrogen, phosphorus and potassium. The only chemical here with any of these in is ammonia. The formula for ammonia is $NH_3$.

**6.** Many substances react with oxygen to form oxides. As a result questions on oxides have appeared in the exam many times.

(a) C + E — 1 mark

**HINT:** Only non-metal oxides will form acidic solutions when dissolved in water. Metal oxides, if they are soluble, will form alkalis.

(b) B — 1 mark

**HINT:** The blast furnace is used to extract iron from iron ore. Iron ore is composed of iron oxide.

(c) E — 1 mark

**HINT:** During a lightening storm there is enough energy from the lightening to make the very unreactive nitrogen gas in the air combine with oxygen to make nitrogen dioxide.

**7.** There is usually a question on the voltage that batteries produce in the exam. The Electrochemical Series is required for these questions.

(a) C — 1 mark

**TOP EXAM TIP:** Remember that the Electrochemical Series is found on p7 of the data booklet.

**HINT:** The larger the gap between metals on the Electrochemical Series, the larger that voltage. Here the largest gap is between magnesium and silver.

(b) D — 1 mark

Page 144

# Worked Answers to Practice Exam D: General Chemistry

> **HINT** No electricity can be produced from an arrangement where the two electrodes are the same metal.

> ★ **8.** This question is about the two sugars, glucose and sucrose. You need to know what they have in common to answer correctly.

B and E                                                                                               **2 marks**

> **HINT** Because this is a 'select a statement' type question, you should go through each option in turn and decide if it is true or false.
>
> - A is incorrect. Glucose ($C_6H_{12}O_6$) and sucrose ($C_{12}H_{22}O_{11}$) both contain oxygen as well as carbon and hydrogen.
> - B is correct. Since glucose and sucrose contain carbon and hydrogen they will burn to produce carbon dioxide and water.
> - C is incorrect. The reaction for photosynthesis is
>   carbon dioxide + water → glucose + oxygen.
>   Glucose is made in this reaction, sucrose is not.
> - D is incorrect. Glucose will turn Benedict's solution from blue to orange but sucrose will not.
> - E is correct. As seen in the formulae given above, both contain the elements carbon, hydrogen and oxygen.

## Part 2 – Written Answers

> ★ **9.** This question tests knowledge of plastics and fuels. The common skill of constructing a table is also tested.

(a)

| Property of nylon (or Property) | Use |
| --- | --- |
| Strong | Climbing ropes |
| Quick Drying | Shirts |
| Hard wearing | Carpets |
| Flexible | Tennis racquet strings |

This table is marked in the following way:
A table is drawn:                                                                                    ½ **mark**
There are suitable headings:                                                                         ½ **mark**
The information is entered correctly into table:                                                     **1 mark**
It does not matter what order the information is entered in.

(b) You must mention the following things for the                                                    **2 marks**.

You get a ½ a **mark** for saying that crude oil is made from animals or tiny sea creatures. Another ½ a **mark** is for suggesting that it happened millions of years ago. It is not acceptable to say that it happened either a long time ago or that it was thousands of years ago.

For the **second mark** you must have 2 of the following:

- A mention of the creatures being buried.

## Worked Answers to Practice Exam D: General Chemistry

- A mention that the creatures rot or decay or turn into oil.
- A mention of pressure and heat being needed (saying squashed or crushed and heated would be ok).

**HINT:** Remember that oil is made from animals or tiny sea creatures and coal is made from plants. It is easy to get them mixed up.

(c) Able to rot away or decay. **1 mark**

It is acceptable to write that it is able to decompose. Any mention of corrosion (corroding) or erosion (eroding) will be marked wrong.

**TOP EXAM TIP:** Be careful when answering a question involving biodegradable. You are just as likely to be asked what non-biodegradable means in an exam. Make sure you are certain which they have asked and that your answer matches this.

**10.** Questions based on cracking are common in the General exam. In part (c) knowledge from the plastics topic is needed.

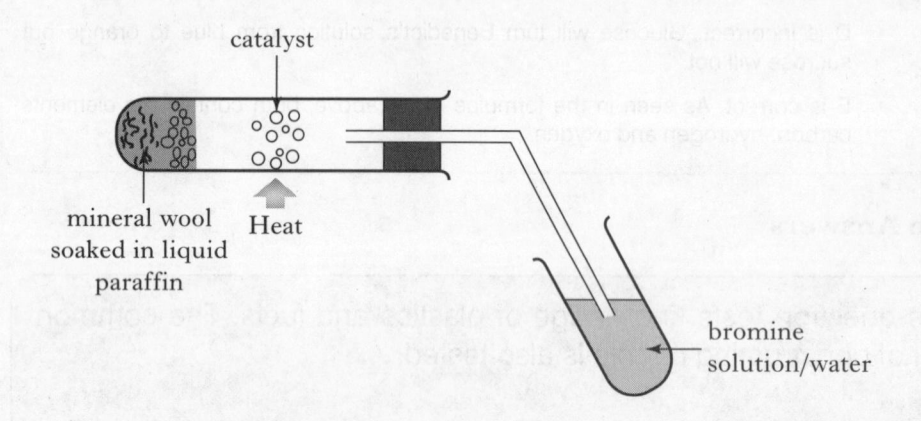

(a) [Diagram: test tube with mineral wool soaked in liquid paraffin, catalyst, heated, with delivery tube leading to bromine solution/water] **1 mark**

**HINT:** Bromine water is the test for unsaturated hydrocarbons. If you are asked to describe the test then you should describe the colour change as 'the bromine water is decolourised rapidly'. 'Rapidly' should be used because even alkanes will decolourise bromine water if left for long enough, especially if they are left in the light.

(b) (i)

[Structural formula: H-C-C-C-C-C-H with H atoms on each carbon, pentane structure]

**HINT:** It is always wise to go back and count the bonds round all the carbons. Make sure each carbon has 4 bonds and each hydrogen has only one bond.

(ii) $C_7H_{16}$ **1 mark**

**HINT:** When an alkane is cracked it breaks into two or more molecules. However, the number of carbon and hydrogen atoms will not change overall. Make sure that the numbers of carbons and hydrogens are the same on both sides.
e.g. $C_5 + C_2 = C_7$, and $H_{12} + H_4 = H_{16}$

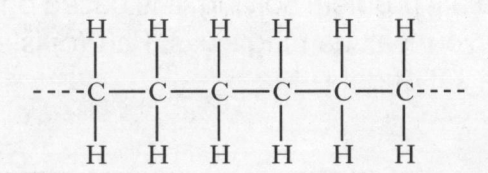

# Worked Answers to Practice Exam D: General Chemistry

(c)

```
    H   H   H   H   H   H
    |   |   |   |   |   |
----C---C---C---C---C---C----
    |   |   |   |   |   |
    H   H   H   H   H   H
```

**1 mark**

**HINT:** The section must contain six carbon atoms and 12 hydrogen atoms. The carbon atoms must be linked by **single** bonds. A common mistake is to keep the double bonds between the carbons. When the ethene monomers join together, the carbon-to-carbon double bonds open up.

---

**11.** This question is based around three different chemical reactions and covers aspects from across the course.

---

(a) One **1 mark**

**HINT:** There are several signs of a chemical reaction. They include a colour change, a state change and an energy change. A chemical reaction may show one, two or three of these but there must be at least one new substance made.

(b) (i) Fermentation anaerobic respiration is also an acceptable answer

**1 mark**

**HINT:** Fermentation is used to make alcohol from glucose using enzymes in yeast as the catalyst.

(ii) Covalent **1 mark**

**HINT:** Covalent bonds are formed between non-metal atoms. If a metal is joined to a non-metal then the bonding is ionic.

(c) Mercury oxide → mercury + oxygen **1 mark**

**HINT:** The elements that make up mercury oxide are mercury and oxygen. When the mercury oxide is heated it breaks up into these elements.

**TOP EXAM TIP**
When writing **word** equations make sure that you do not have any chemical symbols. Only use words.

## Worked Answers to Practice Exam D: General Chemistry

> **12.** This question is mainly problem solving. It is based on hydrochloric acid. Part (b) tests your salt naming skills. Part (c) is about making a prediction from a set of data

(a)

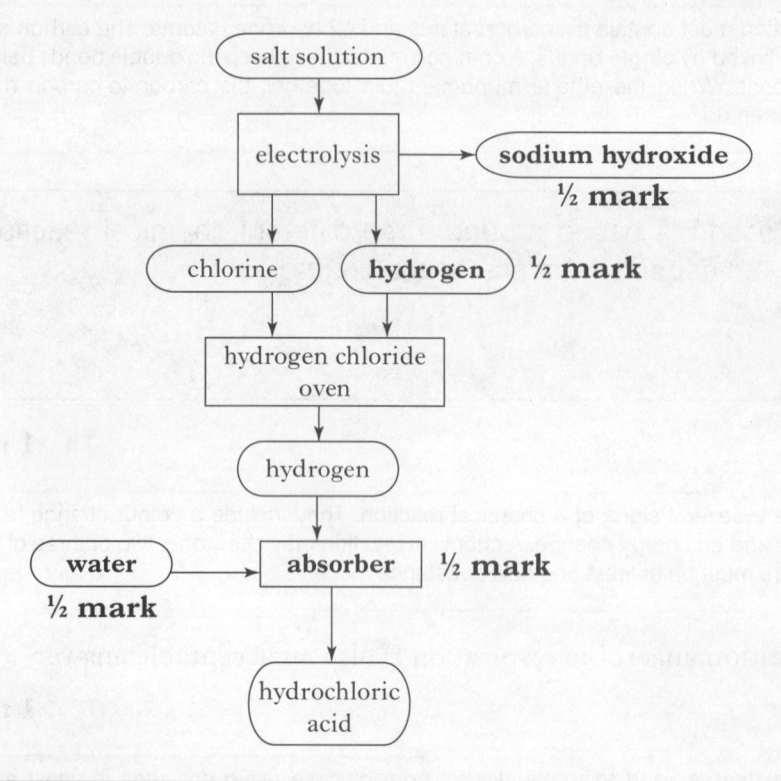

```
                    salt solution
                          │
                          ▼
                    ┌───────────┐
                    │electrolysis│ ──────▶ **sodium hydroxide**
                    └───────────┘              ½ mark
                      │       │
                      ▼       ▼
                  chlorine  **hydrogen**   ½ mark
                      │       │
                      ▼       ▼
                  ┌──────────────────┐
                  │ hydrogen chloride│
                  │      oven        │
                  └──────────────────┘
                          │
                          ▼
                      hydrogen
                          │
       water ──────▶ ┌─────────┐   ½ mark
       ½ mark        │absorber │
                     └─────────┘
                          │
                          ▼
                   hydrochloric
                       acid
```

**HINT**
Look at the two different shapes of box in the chart.

◯ contains the name of chemicals

▭ contains the name of a reactor or process

This should help you to fill in the chart.

(b) Potassium chloride                                               **1 mark**

**HINT**
When naming a salt the first part of the name comes from the neutraliser and the second part comes from the acid. The following table will help, using the acid to name the second part of the name of the salt:

| Acid        | Second Part of the Name |
|-------------|-------------------------|
| hydrochloric | chloride               |
| nitric      | nitrate                 |
| sulphuric   | sulphate                |

In this case potassium oxide is the neutraliser.

**TOP EXAM TIP**
Often in the general exam you will be asked to make a prediction. Try to find a pattern between the numbers given. Work out the difference between the values that you are given. Use this to give you an idea of what the answer is.

(c) Between 100 and 102°C                                            **1 mark**

Worked Answers to Practice Exam D: General Chemistry

**13.** This question is based on the reaction of metals with water. It also tests your knowledge of alkalis.

(a) Hydrogen **1 mark**

(b) (i) Add a few drops of universal indicator **or** dip the pH paper into the solution. **½ mark**

Compare the colour to a pH colour chart to get the pH of the solution. **½ mark**

**HINT** You must say that you will use a pH colour chart. Without this it is not possible to tell what the exact pH is.

(ii) Hydroxide **or** OH⁻ **1 mark**

**HINT** All alkalis have the hydroxide ion (OH⁻) in them. All acids contain the hydrogen ion (H⁺).

(c) Sink **1 mark**

**HINT** Look up the density in the data booklet. The density of calcium (1.54 g/cm³) is more that 1.00 g/cm³ so it will sink.

**14.** This question is based on zinc. It tests your problem solving skills as you need to draw a bar chart and label a pie chart. There are also two corrosion questions.

(a)

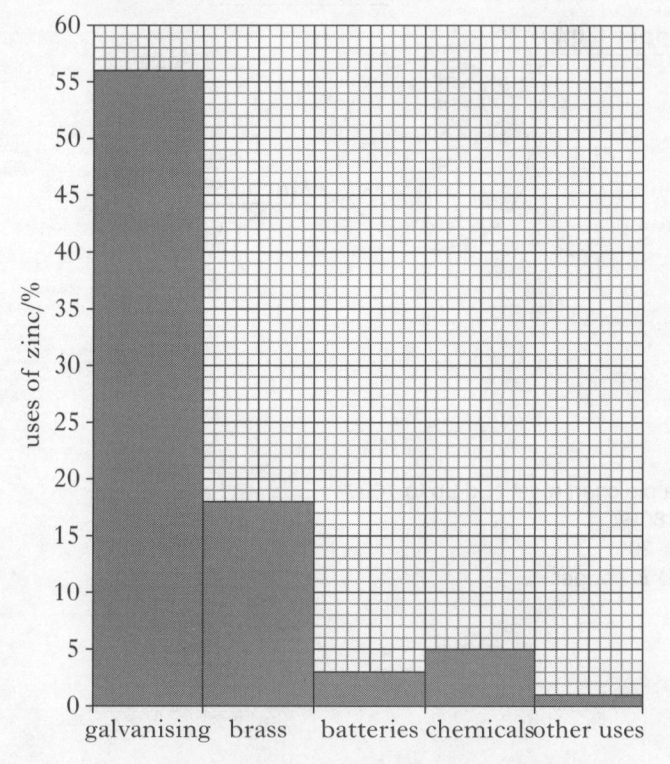

*Page 149*

## Worked Answers to Practice Exam D: General Chemistry

The bar graph is marked in this way:

Uses of zinc labelled on *x*-axis and all bars labelled:  
½ mark

You have a vertical scale on the *y*-axis: ½ mark

The bars are drawn at the correct height: 1 mark

**TOP EXAM TIP**
When drawing bar charts it is very important to make sure your graph is as clearly and accurately drawn as possible: use as much space as you can to draw the graph, label the axes, create a vertical scale on the y axis and, of course, get the bars at the right height

(b) (i) Either, the zinc provides a protective layer stopping oxygen and water coming into contact with the iron **or** the zinc provides the iron with electrons **or** the zinc provides sacrificial protection.  **1 mark**

**HINT:** Iron rusts when it comes into contact with oxygen and water. The iron loses electrons to the oxygen and water. This means that there are two main ways of protecting iron from rusting. You can provide a physical barrier to stop oxygen and water coming into contact with the iron. You can also give iron electrons so that any it loses are replaced immediately. Because zinc is higher in the electrochemical series than iron, it can give iron electrons.

(ii) Any one from
- painting
- oil/greasing
- covering with plastic
- electroplating
- tin-plating
- sacrificial protection (or description of connecting iron to metal higher in electrochemical series)
- cathodic protection (or description of connecting iron to negative terminal of battery). **1 mark**

(c)

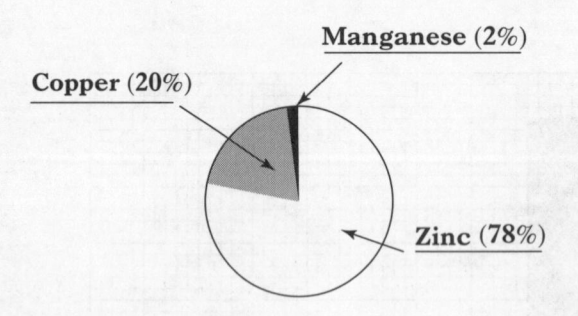

Manganese (2%)
Copper (20%)
Zinc (78%)

Copper ½ mark
20% ½ mark
Manganese 2% ½ mark
Zinc 78% ½ mark

**HINT:** The parts of a pie chart must add up to 100%.
78% + 2% = 80%
100% − 80% = 20%
Therefore 20% is copper.

Page 150

# Worked Answers to Practice Exam D: General Chemistry

> **15.** This question is based on the fertilisers topic. There is a formula to work out here too.

(a) (i) Platinum  **1 mark**

> **HINT** The two industrial processes you need to know about are the Haber process to make ammonia (uses an iron catalyst) and the Ostwald process to make nitric acid from ammonia (uses a platinum catalyst). You should know what each makes and the catalyst for each.

(ii) NO  **1 mark**

> **HINT** You should know when to use the number prefix that allows you to get the formula from the name of a compound and know what each prefix is. In this case nitrogen **mon**oxide, the prefix **mono** means **one**. **Mon**oxide means **one** oxygen.

(b) The plants can absorb the nitrogen in the nitrates **or** adds nitrogen to the soil.  **1 mark**

> **HINT** You need to know the three essential elements for healthy plant growth. These are nitrogen (N), phosphorus (P) and potassium (K).

> **16.** This question is based around everyday uses for neutralisation. Part (c) asks you to write a molecular formula from a full structural formula.

(a) (i) The pH increases or the acidity decreases **or** the pH moves towards 7.  **1 mark**

> **HINT** Acids have a pH less than 7. The lower the pH, the stronger the acid. When acid is neutralised it brings the pH towards 7. This is an increase in pH number and a decrease in acidity.

(ii) Carbon dioxide  **1 mark**

> **HINT** When a neutraliser contains carbon (i.e. a carbonate) then it will release carbon dioxide when it reacts.

(b) $C_5H_{12}O_5$  **1 mark**

> **HINT** The order of the elements is not important. You must have the number of elements as a subscript (little number positioned low after the symbol).

**17.** This question is based on fuels. In part (b) you need to look at experimental results and describe a trend. You also need to know about fair tests.

(a) Fractional distillation  **1 mark**

*HINT:* To separate crude oil into fractions you must say that you use **fractional** distillation.

(b) (i) It decreases (gets shorter).  **1 mark**

*HINT:* When answering a question that asks about a trend or pattern look for a general pattern. Do not describe each number in detail.

**TOP EXAM TIP**
Try not to use the word 'amount' when describing variables. Use words such as volume, mass etc.

(ii) Volume of oil.  **1 mark**

**18.** This question is about the conductivity of elements and compounds. It shows experimental instructions in the form of a workcard. This format is sometimes used in the General exam.

(a) The bulb would light.  **1 mark**
(b) Electrons  **1 mark**

**TOP EXAM TIP**
Learn the rules for conductivity

*HINT:* Charged particles carry the current when a substance conducts. In metals (including wires) it is electrons that flow. In ionic solutions it is the ions that flow.

(c) Non-metal  **(½ mark)**
    Non-conductor  **(½ mark)**

*HINT:* The rule for elements conducting electricity is:
All metals conduct electricity. All non-metals do not, except carbon in the form of graphite.

(d) Its ions are not free to move.  **1 mark**

**TOP EXAM TIP**
You should check over all your answers once you finish the paper. Don't leave any blanks. Always attempt to write something for each question.

*HINT:* When an ionic compound conducts its ions must be free to move to carry the current. In a solid ionic compound the ions are held in a fixed position in a lattice.